CAVIAR

MITCHELL BEAZLEY

CAVIAR

SUSIE BOECKMANN & NATALIE REBEIZ-NIELSEN

Photographs by Jason Lowe

Caviar by Susie Boeckmann &
Natalie Rebeiz-Nielson
First published in Great Britain by
Mitchell Beazley, an imprint of the
Octopus Publishing Group Limited,
2-4 Heron Quays, London E14 4JP

Commissioning Editor: Margaret Little
Art Director: Gaye Allen
Executive Art Editor: Tracy Killick
Managing Editor: Lucy Bridgers
Editors: Mandy Greenfield, Gill Pitts
Photography: Jason Lowe
Production: Karen Farquhar

Printed and bound in China
by Toppan Printing Co.(H.K.) Ltd.

ISBN: 1 84000 177 1

A CIP catalogue record of this book is
available from the British Library

CONTENTS

AUTHOR'S NOTE

We have taken every possible care to verify our sources and the information received from all over the world, but the caviar industry is rife with conflicting stories and likes to keep its myths and secrets intact. We cannot, therefore, vouch for the accuracy of all the information included in this book.

We have avoided giving prices, as the circumstances may change considerably in the foreseeable future due to the growth of sturgeon farming and the fact that the wild species is endangered. It is also impossible to give accurate figures for the amount and sturgeon currently being caught and caviar being processed as the industry is very fragmented. States bordering the Caspian Sea keep their information strictly confidential and, obviously, all the illegal sturgeon fishing is unrecorded.

ACKNOWLEDGEMENTS

Special thanks must go to Georges Rebeiz, the king of caviar! Who started it all. Caviar House – who has given us so much background information and advice; allowed us total access to their archives from the beginning to the present and have showed enormous patience with all our questions and requests. Musée Océanographique de Monaco – thanks to Madame Damiano and her team in the library for their patient and resourceful searches into anything on sturgeon and caviar written from the beginning of the century until now. And it was such a marvellous place to work! Dr. Alan Jones in Bordeaux – he and his team are breeding more baby sturgeon than any other aquaculturist and his world-wide experience is of enormous value to the survival of the species. The Iranian State Fisheries (SHILAT) for their patient help and assistance. Ingrid Millet for an insight into their superbly constructed beauty products based with caviar. Paula Bartholdy for her help in testing many of the recipes. Professor Alwyn Wheeler, formerly of the British Museum (Natural History) whose expertize in the world of whales and sturgeon is invaluable. The World Wildlife Fund. Mogens Nielsen for his help with the wine recommendations. Finally, a big thank you to the team at Mitchell Beazley for giving us such wonderful support – to Margaret Little for taking us on and making things happen; to our editors Lucy Bridgers (who also compiled the wine recommendations), Gill Pitts and Mandy Greenfield for their unswerving patience and efficiency; to Gaye Allen and Tracy Killick for making the book look utterly gorgeous; and to Jason Lowe for his stunning photography. Other pictures copyright: Caviar House 8-9, 11, 14, 16-17, 32 left.

INTRODUCTION

Caviar – food of the gods and relished by lesser mortals too. For centuries the salted roe of the sturgeon has been highly prized and treasured by the great and the good. Ancient Phoenicians used it to sustain them in times of war and famine; Pliny and Ovid sung its praises in their verse; and the Russian Tsars and Emperors of Manchuria reserved it greedily and wisely for themselves. To this day, caviar remains undoubtedly the most sought-after, exquisite delicacy in the world and it is certainly the most exclusive.

Caviar is a totally natural, complete food. It is derived from a fish that ranges enormously in individual species, age and habitat. Today it is available in a bewildering range of quality, colour and flavour. A key question in many peoples' minds is often which variety of caviar is the best. To professionals in the caviar business, this is rather like asking whether you prefer sole, salmon or trout – it all depends on personal preference, mood, circumstances. Perhaps your dealer has better Oscietre than Sevruga in stock, or vice versa. Many claim that a black Beluga with large eggs is the best; others insist that a grey egg is the only good colour. In reality there is no difference in the quality – the colour of the eggs depends on the individual fish. Beluga is certainly the rarest and this makes is the most expensive, but not necessarily "the best". Many professionals prize new-season Sevruga above all others. The French, who are great consumers of caviar eat the most Oscietre, while older generations, Eastern Europeans and Russians prefer pressed caviar.

Above all, caviar is about pure pleasure. It is about spoiling yourself, indulging and relaxing with one of the most sensual, irresistable, exquisite tastes in life.

CAVIAR THROUGH THE AGES

Before the revolution they were loyal to the Tsar,
Those death-defying Cossacks who much enjoyed their power
They played the balalaika and threw glasses in the fire,
They wore fur hats, smart boots and dined on caviar.

LADY RICE

A LOOK BACK
IN TIME

He who eateth caviales eateth salt,
dung and flies.

17TH CENTURY ITALIAN PROVERB

The sturgeon existed in prehistoric times – fossil remains have been found on the Baltic coast – and, broadly speaking, its form hasn't changed since the Jurassic period (circa 180 million BC). The fish is a primitive "living fossil", with a largely cartilaginous skeleton, that is, it has little bone. The flesh of the sturgeon has been appreciated as a food for many centuries, but it is only since the 1500s that its eggs have been considered as a delicacy.

Around 2400 BC ancient Egyptian and, subsequently, Phoenician coastal dwellers would salt and pickle both fish and eggs to sustain them during periods of war, famine or long sea voyages. Bas-reliefs at the Necropolis at Ti, near the Saqquarah Pyramid in Egypt, show fishermen catching a variety of fish, gutting them and removing their eggs. Coins dating from 600 BC from Carthage, the ancient Phoenician port in present-day Tunisia, depict a sturgeon, while in 400 BC the capital of the Bosphorian kingdom, Pantikopey, minted copper coins that also featured the fish.

GREEK AND ROMAN EULOGIES

In the 2nd century BC the Greek rhetorician Claudius Aelianus eulogized the Beluga sturgeon of the Balkan Danube when describing his "recent voyages". He wrote of catching the sturgeon with special hooks on lines that were attached to a rope stretched across the river. The Belugas were so big and heavy that bullocks and horses were used to help pull in the

lines and nets. According to ancient manuscripts, the fish were so highly prized that in Athens a single amphora, or jar, of sturgeon was more expensive than a whole *hectatomba* (equivalent to 100 sheep or one bull). When the Roman Empire was at the height of its prosperity (from the 4th century BC onwards) many of its writers and philosophers wrote about sturgeon. Aristotle (384–322 BC) stated that sturgeon was delicious. He also described how a gelatine made from the fish's swim-bladder was used as a strong glue; it was used for clarifying wine as well (today the gelatine is known as isinglass). Cicero (106–43 BC) bemoaned the exorbitant cost of

Above: The roe is very carefully extracted from the female fish and the eggs are passed through a horse hair sieve. This removes the membrane and separates the eggs.

having sturgeon at banquets, while the poet Ovid (43 BC–17 AD) depicted the sturgeon as a fish of noble character. Pliny the Elder (23–79 AD) wrote that whole sturgeon, decorated with garlands of flowers, were brought to the table at banquets, accompanied by musicians playing flutes and trumpets, and, if the Greek writer Atheneus is to be believed, sturgeon flesh was still the favourite food at important festivals and banquets in the 2nd century AD. Furthermore, Roman remains in Wales have revealed evidence of sturgeon farming in the farther-flung outposts of the Roman empire.

MEDIEVAL MENUS

In 1240 Batu Khan (the grandson of Genghis Khan, c. 1162–1227, who was known – apart from his conquering exploits – as the man who travelled all day with chunks of meat between his horse and saddlebags to tenderize them) was honoured by a feast at a monastery on the banks of the River Volga. The menu began with fish soup made from Sterlet, and included a large roasted sturgeon, eel pâté, *pirozhki* (pies) stuffed with finely chopped mushrooms, followed by crystallized apples and caviar.

Between 1236 and 1246 Batu Khan conquered southern Russia and all the lands surrounding the Black and Caspian Seas. The Tartars built log barriers, known as *uchugi*, across the Volga's tributaries – the *uchugi* had hooks on top to catch sturgeon when they migrated upstream. In 1554 Ivan the Terrible (1530–84) drove the Tartars out, and from then until the mid-20th century sturgeon fishing in the Volga and Caspian was under Russian control. In 1675 Tsar Alexei I Mikhailovitch (1629–76) declared Russia's exclusive authority to market caviar, and 20 years later Peter the Great (1672–1725) established the first fishing bureau in Astrakhan.

During the Middle Ages large shoals of sturgeon would migrate up many of the main rivers of Europe, including the Thames in England, the Seine and Gironde in France, the Po in Italy, the Ebro and Guadalquivir in Spain, and the upper stretches of the Danube. In Germany sturgeon were so prolific that it was written into employment contracts that the workers would not have to eat the fish more than twice a week. Yet sturgeon were still highly valued – sovereigns of various countries such as Russia, China, Germany, Denmark, France and England claimed the rights both to this fish and whales, so fishermen were obliged to offer their catch to the sovereign, often for fixed rewards.

"FISHES ROYAL"

Henry II of England (1133–89) placed sturgeon under royal protection. Then, during the 14th century Edward II (1284–1327) passed an edict on "fishes royal" – a copy of which still exists in the Royal Windsor Library. On the rare occasions when sturgeon are caught in British waters today, the monarch still retains the first right to the fish (although the fishermen have often been allowed to keep it, once it has been offered).

Beluga sturgeon have been known to swallow salmon whole. There have also been reports of aquatic birds, baby seals and even a horse's head being found in a Beluga's stomach.

In 1165 Alfonso II of Aragón made fishing in the River Ebro free to his subjects, but retained his regal right to the sturgeon. In France, *le droit d'esturgeon* meant that the ownership of all sturgeon caught in an area bordered by the Seine and Rhône rivers was constituted a privilege reserved for the aristocracy and the high clergy, as decreed by the King. And during the 17th century the renowned Minister of Finance, Jean-Baptiste Colbert (1619–83), brought in special regulations to protect the sturgeon, which remain in force to this day.

COSSACKS' PRIVILEGE

In Russia and Hungary, parts of the rivers that attracted Beluga sturgeon were the subject of special royal grants. Under the Tsars' patronage, and provided they paid a large tax in kind to them, Cossacks were allowed to fish the Dnieper, Don and Ural rivers for sturgeon for a fortnight twice a year, in spring and autumn. The early spring catch (*bagornaya*) was made under the ice: a stretch of river would be surrounded by Cossacks armed with harpoons, and when a cannon was fired everyone would make a hole in the ice and try to harpoon the sturgeon beneath which had become agitated due to the noise. As each part of the river was fished, the Cossacks moved downstream until they reached the river's mouth. During the autumn catch (*plawnaya*), the entire family would camp by the river as hundreds of participating Cossacks gradually pulled the driftnets down the river, entangling the sturgeon as they went.

Below: The sturgeon roe is being prepared for pressing. Here the roe is soaking in brine.

Apart from the Cossacks and their families, the river banks were crowded with rich dealers from Moscow, St Petersburg and other European cities, who followed the fishermen down the rivers in their carriages or sleighs. The freshly caught sturgeon were sold to the highest bidder, who then had the fish killed. The caviar was prepared on the spot, then packed in barrels filled with ice, ready to be transported by bullock cart and later by rail.

The Cossacks continued to hold the right to sturgeon fishing under Tsar Nicholas II (1868–1918), who took the tax in kind, since he was extremely fond of caviar and put great faith in its health benefits. This practice was put to an end with the advent of the Russian Revolution in 1917.

THE CAVIAR TRADE

Caviar has been traded for many centuries. However, it was only in 1820 that a private caviar company in Moscow named Sapozhnikov Brothers introduced the use of refrigeration. This revolutionized storage and so increased production. It also led to a much lower salt content as less was needed as a preservative. Caviar tins as we know them today were first used around 1918–22, although the first tins had been patented in the United States in 1875.

There are several long-established companies around the world that have imported caviar from Russia and Iran. Of these, several have interesting histories that have involved crossing traditional trade boundaries, in spite of wars, economics and politics. The best-known companies were established either at the turn of the 20th century or shortly after the Russian Revolution in 1917. Several importers and restaurateurs then set up shop in Paris which, since their second language was French, proved a natural place for Russian émigrés to settle after fleeing the Revolution. Some, such as Caviar Kaspia, are still thriving today in Paris and London. The Petrossian family are split between London and New York and there are several other long-established companies in Germany and New York. Caviar House was established by Georges Rebeiz in 1950. He gained invaluable knowledge of the subject from the legendary Russian caviar producer Oyzanov – colloquially known as "Mr Caspian Sea". The company is now run from Geneva, London and Copenhagen by his children.

Overleaf: Large barrels such as these were used for storing caviar which would have been pressed before transportation.

THE
CAVIAR
CATCH

*There is more simplicity in
the man who eats caviar on
impulse than in the man
who eats grape-nuts on
principle.*

G.K. CHESTERTON

HARVESTING
THE WATERS

Traditionally, in the Caspian Sea, children play with baby sturgeon. The fish become quite tame in aquariums and will come up to be stroked.

There are several species of sturgeon distributed in the seas and rivers of the northern hemisphere (*see* chart on p34). To complicate things, many types of sturgeon cross-breed, which makes identification rather difficult, with even the experts disagreeing. However, the key species as far as caviar connoisseurs are concerned are Beluga, Oscietre and Sevruga, found in the Black, Azov and Caspian Seas. It is the unique combination of temperature, natural habitat and water conditions that gives caviar from Caspian Sea sturgeons its indisputably fine flavour – considered the best in the world.

THE CASPIAN SEA

In prehistoric times the Caspian Sea was linked to the Arctic Ocean; today it is the largest inland salt-water lake in the world. Its statistics are staggering: approximately 400,000 sq km (155,000 sq miles) in area, 1,200 km (750 miles) in length, and 200–560 km (125–350 miles) in width. Of the Caspian's lengthy coastline, approximately one-third is controlled by Iran and the remaining two-thirds by Russia, Azerbaijan, Kazakhstan and Turkmenistan.

The water that supplies the Caspian comes mainly from the many rivers that flow into it, the most important being the Volga, which provides over half its volume. The northern end of the sea is shallow and varies in depth from 4 to 25 m (13–82 ft); the southern end is much deeper, varying between 250 and 900 m (820–2,950 ft), and is fed by underwater streams. And yet, in spite of all this fresh water, the sea maintains an average salinity of around 10 per cent. The sea temperature in the northern waters of the Caspian in January is 0°C (32°F), in the central areas 5–10°C (41–50°F) and in the southern part 10–20°C (50–68°F). By July the temperature in the south is around 20–25°C (68–77°F).

The southern part of the Caspian Sea is much less polluted than its northern areas, as Iran has little heavy industry around its coastline, unlike the Volga delta in the north. This area has a horrendous history of giant industrial projects, damming and agricultural irrigation plants, which have resulted in pollution, clogged-up river beds and, most seriously, the destruction of many of the sturgeon's traditional spawning areas.

It is said that the reason Russia converted to Christianity in the 10th century was because the Tsar had to choose between the Moslem religion and Christianity. He was very fond of vodka and, therefore, since alcohol was forbidden in the Moslem religion, he decreed that Russia would embrace Christianity.

Like salmon, most species of sturgeon return from the sea to their birth river to spawn but, unlike most salmon, a sturgeon can spawn many times in its lifetime (some fish have been recorded as living for 170 years or more). The female normally likes to lay her eggs in fairly shallow water on stony or gravel river beds. However, she has the ability to keep the eggs inside her for up to two or three years, if the conditions for spawning are not suitable.

Unlike salmon, the sturgeon (which primarily lives on the bottom of the sea) cannot jump high enough to return upstream via the high dam walls that have been built at the northern end of the Caspian. Attempts to provide "ladders" to enable the fish to return upriver have not been a success. The water level in the Caspian changes fairly frequently and, after dropping continuously for a number of years, suddenly rose by several metres in 1994. As a result, most of the fishing stations were flooded, as were many of the oil installations, which in turn added to the pollution; by 1998 this had led to a 40 per cent drop in the catch by the Iranian fisheries. The biggest polluter in the Caspian is the oil business, with its old, decaying installations and the constant exploration for new oil fields – so vital to the economies of Caspian countries.

Below: At Iranian fishing stations on the Caspian Sea the nets have to be carefully maintained. These methods have not changed for hundreds of years.

Another important factor in the fall in sturgeon numbers in the Caspian is overfishing. As a result of this stocks declined severely at the beginning of the 20th century, and so from then until the First World War the Russians reduced fishing in their rivers. This was extremely effective and improved stocks enormously. Unfortunately by 1930 the gains were all but lost due to new fishing methods. Between 1925 and 1930 long-line fishing was introduced, in which the total length of sturgeon nets exceeded 10,000 km

(6,215 miles). Nets were left in the sea for most of the year, blocking the migratory fish from their traditional feeding and spawning grounds. Many of the long lines and nets were unattended, causing enormous wastage of fish, which either died on the hooks or freed themselves, only to die later. During 1902–7 an average of over 40 tonnes per annum of Beluga sturgeon was caught; the last official Beluga catch figure from the USSR (in 1990) was only 8 tonnes per annum – a figure that is still decreasing rapidly.

The Beluga is now in danger of extinction if protective measures cannot be enforced to control the situation. Since 1988, the catch of Oscietre and Sevruga has stayed at around 400–450 and 600–650 tonnes respectively. The Sterlet, common until the 1940s, hardly exists as a commercial fish today, but it does play a valuable role in artificial propagation programmes.

In 1993 a 5.2 m (17 ft) long sturgeon (Kaluga) was caught in the Amur River in China. It was described as being as big as a mini-bus.

Poaching and illegal fishing are also playing havoc with sturgeon stocks. The sheer volume of indiscriminate fishing is leading to an enormous amount of waste. Too often the fish are incorrectly caught, badly processed and generally handled by people who are ignorant of the great art of caviar making – but not of the high prices caviar commands.

RUSSIAN AND IRANIAN CAVIAR

Russia used to have the reputation for producing the best caviar in the world. In 1893 the Russians made an agreement with Iran to purchase, process and import all the Iranian sturgeon catch, which resulted in the Iranians being forced to sell to the Russians at vastly reduced prices. For 60 years negotiations continued, mainly to the benefit of "Mighty Russia" (even after the Russian state fisheries were nationalized in 1928). That said, Russia's financial and technical contributions did help to modernize and organize the Iranian fishing stations. Finally in 1952 when the then Iranian prime minister, Dr Mohammed Mosadegh, came to power, the treaty was ended by both parties who agreed fishing rights and became independent of each other.

Right: The fishermen's catch is approved by an inspector who confirms the age and sex of the fish. He then feels the sturgeon's stomach to see how full of eggs it is – if there are not enough the fish is thrown back into the water.

Since the dissolution of the USSR in the late 1980s there has been an almost complete breakdown in control of the previously strict quotas on sturgeon catches. It is no longer the state that controls the caviar market, ensuring that the eggs are produced in prime condition. Today, with the USSR divided into individual states, anyone with a small boat can go fishing for sturgeon. This has led to a great deal of poaching and over-fishing; the local police (who are generally poorly paid) are often rewarded with some sturgeon if they attempt to confiscate the catch from the fishermen. The caught fish might be immature and so have no eggs, and even if a mature female is killed it may be some time before the roe is removed. There is often no proper hygiene or special knowledge of caviar processing – the eggs are not properly handled or cleaned – so it is often dangerous to consume the caviar, as without the correct conditions harmful bacteria will reach dangerous levels. Unfortunately, the eggs are sold in fake tins or are labelled to resemble the official state packaging.

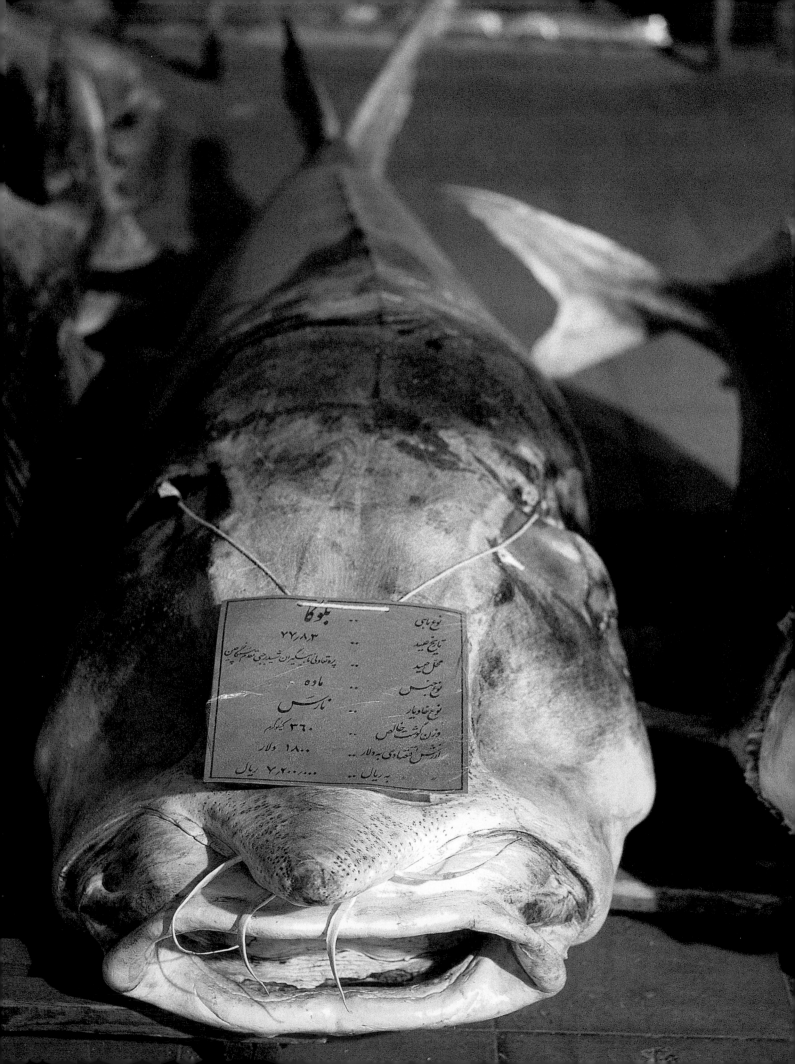

If you buy illegal caviar "on the street", you really have no idea how it has been processed or whether it has been kept at the correct temperature. Previously all tins of caviar produced by the USSR had a code indicating where and when the fish had been caught, with a batch number marking the individual eggs from each fish. Now, because caviar has become such a valuable commodity, powerful mafia groups have muscled in and virtually control the fishing stations in many areas. Payments are in cash and many drug barons have switched to trading in caviar since it is considered less dangerous. Nevertheless, in 1996 30 people were killed when an apartment block near Moscow was blown up by mafiosi during the so-called "caviar wars".

Today, a staggering 80 per cent of the Caspian catch is offered by irregular sources in the surrounding countries. Iran is the exception – it has thoroughly re-organized its caviar industry, made firm contracts with its international customers and cut out nearly all illegal fishing. As a result, Iran is generally producing a better product than the other Caspian countries, although professional buyers who have been visiting Russia for many years still know exactly where to go to buy traditional quality caviar.

Left: This 2 m (6 ft) long Beluga was caught by Iranian fishermen and has been reserved for scientific research. It is estimated to have been between 70 and 90 years old.

CONSERVATION AND THE FUTURE

With the serious decline in traditional sturgeon stocks, it is essential that steps are taken to preserve this ancient species in whatever form is viable. Unfortunately the various ecological, political and economic situations in the Caspian are often incompatible with conservation. If we are to believe the information emanating from Caspian sources, the situation is now at crisis point. Until a concerted effort is made by all the countries and parties concerned to protect the sturgeon and allow stocks to reproduce naturally (or through farming and ranching), to limit fishing to certain times of the year and to control fishing equipment (such as the size of nets and boats), then this species is in grave danger of extinction. Some scientists believe that the only natural way to allow the sturgeon to recover is to ban fishing altogether in the sea and restrict it to the rivers. Yet this would be hard to enforce due to the immediate impact it would have on the livelihood of the Caspian fishermen and others involved in the caviar industry.

However, for several years the main caviar importers in Europe have been working towards bringing in controls and have forged an agreement to try to protect and regulate the sturgeon industry. According to in-depth research by the WWF (World Wide Fund for Nature), 24 species of sturgeon have been listed as severely endangered (especially the Beluga), mainly due to overfishing and the huge, worldwide illegal trade in caviar (official Iranian sources aside, 80 per cent of the caviar market is "unofficial").

The Federal Republic of Germany and the US proposed that sturgeon be included in CITES (Convention on International Trade in Endangered Species of Wild Fauna and Flora), which monitors trade through a system of permits. Both Europe and the US agreed to this and, since April 1998, it has been illegal to import, export or re-export caviar without the necessary permit, as well as the relevant veterinary and customs documents. Even private individuals must carry a permit if they are travelling across international borders with more than 250 g (9 oz) of caviar. An influential development has been the introduction of DNA testing to ensure the

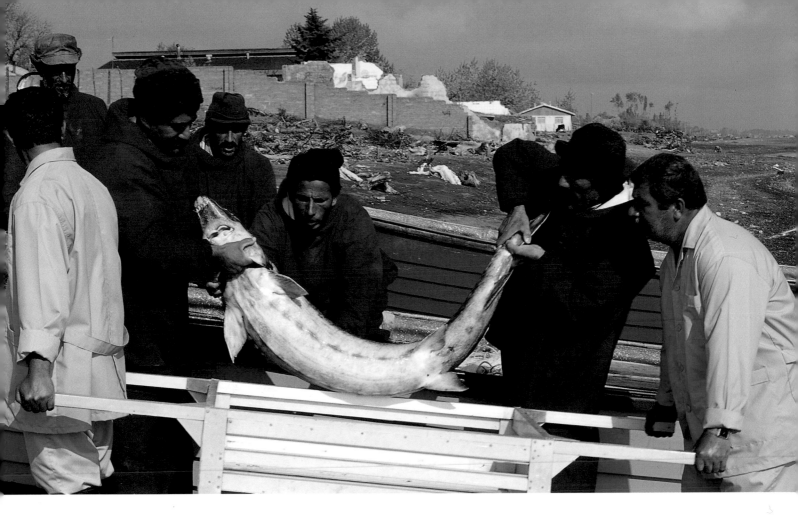

authenticity of the product. Already there have been several test cases in the US where caviar has been confiscated by customs authorities due to irregularities. Apart from being able to identify the type of fish, DNA testing can tell where the caviar comes from, its age, salt content and other details that are important to the consumer.

Despite all this, the future is far from bleak. Many people are now aware of the huge problem of dwindling sturgeon stocks in the Caspian and elsewhere. With modern technology, major advances are being made in the breeding of the species and its re-introduction to the wild. Although caviar never achieves quite the same flavour if it is not sourced from fish in the Caspian (and technically should not be labelled "caviar" unless it comes from that region), many countries are now active in sturgeon farming, realizing that it has a valuable role to play in the survival of this precious fish. In domestic hatcheries with warm-water conditions the sturgeon develop considerably faster than in the wild – the Siberian sturgeon and white sturgeon, for example, will mature at 8 to 10 years instead of 15 to 25 years.

Above: The fishermen carry every sturgeon to the fishing station, handling each one very carefully to avoid damage. The fish shown is a 12-14 year old Sevruga.

It is a long-term project to be involved with caviar production. But we can draw on lessons learned from the enormous progress made with salmon farming and use our waters as beneficially as we use the land for farming. Russia began raising sturgeon in 1869, and between 1870 and 1920 it developed its hatchery technology. Between 1950 and 1990 around 100 million sturgeon fry were released into the Volga River and Caspian Sea each year. Unfortunately all the traditional hatcheries and restocking programmes have now practically stopped because of Russia's economic situation. The other members of the Commonwealth of Independent States bordering the Caspian Sea – Turkmenistan, Kazakstan, Azerbaijan – claim to be attempting methods of conservation, although their economic and political resources are virtually non-existent. Iran, however, realizes the importance of long-term restocking and is actively increasing its hatcheries and releasing hundreds of thousands of sturgeon fry into the Caspian.

It will take many years for the sturgeon population to increase, especially as far as mature, egg-producing females are concerned, and it may be that sturgeon fry have to be hatched elsewhere in the world in order to restock the Caspian. On a more optimistic note, there are thriving sturgeon farms all over the world – including Germany, Hungary, Romania, Italy, France,

Below: Farm produced baby sturgeon, or fry. Every year some three million of these "fingerlings" are released in the Caspian, helping to ensure the survival of the fishing families that live around its coast (centre).

Spain, Portugal, Israel, the US, Chile, Argentina and Uruguay. For example, Germany is breeding several kinds of sturgeon, mainly for their meat (*see below*), including the Beluga. Some countries have developed methods of saving the female sturgeon, such as taking the eggs by Caesarian section and sewing the fish up again afterwards. It is claimed that one US-bred Bester (a cross between a Beluga and a Sterlet) has successfully had seven such operations over a period of 15 years. Unfortunately, this can only be done on a small number of fish as it is both costly and time-consuming. Similarly technology needs to be developed to find a practical way, apart from blood tests, to differentiate between young male and female sturgeons.

The meat of the sturgeon is becoming increasingly popular. It is firm, white and quite dense, with a delicate fresh flavour. It is also high in protein, low in fat and is boneless. In Russia, dried fillets are prepared in spring when the fish are at their best and the climate is dry. The fish have their heads and gills cut off, are covered with salt and spices, then marinated for 24 hours. They are then hung by the tail to dry and coated with saltpetre (a preservative). After 17 to 21 days they are ready to be consumed. The fillets are considered a great delicacy (they are served sliced like smoked salmon), and will last for several months if kept dry and aerated.

Below: Sturgeon sperm ready to be used for artifical propogation.

WORLD DISTRIBUTION OF STURGEONS

Recorded distribution
of sturgeons

SPECIES	LATIN NAME	PLACE OF ORIGIN
EUROPE		
Beluga	Huso huso	Black, Azov & Caspian Seas
Oscietre	A gueldenstaedti	Black, Azov & Caspian Seas
Sevruga	A stellatus	Black, Azov & Caspian Seas
Schipp	A nudiventris	Caspian & Aral Seas
Sterlet	A ruthenus	European & west Siberian rivers
Persian sturgeon	A persicus	Caspian; east coast of Black Sea
Siberian sturgeon	A baeri	Siberian lakes and rivers
European common sturgeon	A sturio	Atlantic coast; Europe; west Asia
Italian sturgeon	A naccarii	Adriatic sea and rivers

SPECIES	LATIN NAME	PLACE OF ORIGIN
CHINA AND JAPAN		
Kaluga	Huso daurius	Amur delta
Chinese sturgeon	A sinensis	Yangtze river system
Yangtze sturgeon	A dabryanus	Yangtze river system
Japanese sturgeon	A kikuchii	Yangtze river system
UNITED STATES		
White sturgeon	A transmontanus	Pacific coast of North America
Atlantic sturgeon	A oxyrhynchus	Atlantic coast of North America
Great Lakes sturgeon	A fulvescens	Great Lakes basin
Green sturgeon	A medirostris	Pacific coast of Asia
Pallid sturgeon	A scaphirhynchus albus	Mississippi & river system
Shortnose sturgeon	A brevirostrum	Atlantic coast of North America
Shovelnose	Scaphirhynchus platorhynchus	Mississippi & river system

In many places it is possible to obtain sturgeon meat fresh, smoked, tinned or frozen. The Lombardy region of northern Italy is a good example of this, producing several hundred tonnes of sturgeon per year, with top hotels and restaurants in Milan often featuring both smoked and fresh sturgeon on their menus.

During the First World War British soldiers reportedly paid out of their own meagre wages for tins of sardines so that they didn't have to eat "fish jam". They were being supplied with pressed caviar and did not think much of it!

THE FRENCH STURGEON INDUSTRY

Caviar has been appreciated by the French for centuries – in the early 1500s François Rabelais, the French author, satirist and gourmet, wrote how delicious sturgeon and caviar were. Today the French still consume around 15 per cent of the total world production. At various times they have had their own thriving caviar industry, and by 1910 the fish were mainly being caught in the River Gironde and the Garonne and Dordogne tributaries. The well-known Paris restaurateur Monsieur Prunier discovered that the eggs were not valued and were often used as eel bait or as fertilizer. He stumbled across this fact when looking for alternative sources of caviar during the Russian Revolution of 1917.

Prunier teamed up with a Russian with the unlikely name of Scott, to start processing caviar. Between them they helped finance and equip fishermen on the Gironde to catch sturgeon, and it was estimated that up to 100 tonnes a year were caught. This proved so successful that by 1921 Prunier was serving caviar in his Paris restaurants that had been prepared and processed just 24 hours previously. (Nowadays experts would say that the unique blending of salt and eggs takes several weeks to mature and bring out the best flavour.) Unfortunately, by the 1940s French caviar production had died out and it was not until 1982, when only a very few sturgeon were found in the Gironde, that the French national fisheries decided to start a protection and breeding programme with the Siberian sturgeon (*Acipenser baeri*, similar to Oscietre) and the common European sturgeon (*A sturio*), which is the native species. France is very strict about which species are to be used for breeding with its native species, and the former is the closest to it. Other countries, however, are not so strict with regard to the preservation of their endemic species.

There are now five main sturgeon farms operating around the Bordeaux area, under the watchful eye of CEMAGRAF (the equivalent of the state fishery), which runs regular checks on genetics, bacteria and conditions of both habitat and fish. The biggest of these farms is successfully raising 600,000–700,000 "fingerlings" (sturgeon fry) for export all over the world, including the Caspian. This is an important factor in the replenishing of sturgeon stocks, and the farm is consulting both Iran and Russia on more modern methods of breeding technology.

It is estimated that by 2002 the French sturgeon industry could be producing 15–20 tonnes of caviar per annum. While the taste is arguably not as fine as that of the Caspian caviar, and the sturgeon are farmed in fresh water, the French believe that their product has a role to play in the market place as a valuable foodstuff. The eggs are black, and similar in size to those of the Oscietre, and the roe is sold as soon as it is processed, so as to be as fresh as possible. At present French caviar is sold through special outlets, such as selected supermarkets, the Prunier Centre in Paris, and wholesale and gourmet delicatessens. The fresh fish market is also growing, and several tonnes of sturgeon meat are processed in various forms – whole fish of about 2.5 kg (5½ lb) for the restaurant trade, fresh fillets from the back part of the fish, smoked sturgeon, and various pâtés and spreads. It is also sold frozen or tinned, ready to eat.

NORTH AMERICAN CAVIAR

Sturgeon were once commonly found in Alaska, the Great Lakes and most of the US, stretching down to California on the west side and New York State on the east. There are seven main kinds of sturgeon in the US waters. The three types most used commercially are the white sturgeon (*Acipenser*

Forth upon the Gitche Gumee,
On the shining Big-Sea-Water,
With his fishing-line of cedar,
Of the twisted bark of cedar,
Forth to catch the sturgeon Nahma,
Mishe-Nahma, King of Fishes,
In his birch canoe exulting
All alone went Hiawatha.

LONGFELLOW, THE SONG OF HIAWATHA

transmontanus), which is the largest, most valued and has the widest habitat geographically; the Atlantic sturgeon (*A oxyrhynchus*), found on the east, from the St Lawrence River right down to the Gulf of Mexico; and the Great Lakes Sturgeon (*A fulvescens*). There is a fourth variety, called the paddlefish, whose eggs are processed for consumption, but this species belongs to a different family of fish called Polyodontides.

Documents from the 17th century show that there was considerable consumption in North America of pickled and cured sturgeon. A large amount was also exported, packed in barrels. In 1634 one William Wood published a work called *New England's Prospect* and wrote: "Sturgeons be all over the country, but best catching of them be on the shoals of Cape Codde and in the rivers of Merrimacke, where much is taken, pickled and brought for England; some of these be 12, 14, 18 foote long." Another report from this time stated that there were so many sturgeon in some rivers that the fish were a dangerous hazard to canoes and other small boats. The oil produced from sturgeon was reputed to make a better lamp oil than whale oil, so the fish became an even more valuable commodity.

Right: These Sevrugas and Oscietre (top) will be cleaned by being hosed down and scrubbed with a hard brush.

Some caviar was produced, but it did not become very popular until the last quarter of the 19th century, when numerous fishing stations were set up on all the major rivers. A caviar boom got underway in North America; it was even said that caviar was given away free in bars in the years before Prohibition because, being so salty, it would encourage greater consumption of alcohol. In the Delaware River alone, at the peak of the boom, caviar production reached 670 tonnes per year. By 1897, when the sturgeon stocks in the Delaware were becoming too low, fishing rose dramatically on the Fraser River in Vancouver. The record production there was 516 tonnes in one year.

From the late 19th century onwards, shipping caviar to Europe became a highly lucrative business. In 1895 the quantity of North American caviar exported to Germany was at least equal to that produced by Russia. Unfortunately the eggs were smaller, very salty, with less flavour and did not keep well, since pasteurization was only beginning to be used in the US

and Canada around this time. Much of the North American caviar was repackaged in Europe in Russian-style tins and labelled as "Astrakhan caviar". Naturally, this was not appreciated by the authentic caviar producers of Astrakhan, who traditionally produced some of the finest caviar available.

Today there are stringent laws in most American states concerning the catching of sturgeon. This is complicated by the fact that although it is legal to catch some species, it is illegal to process and sell the eggs. Many natural spawning sites and migratory routes have been destroyed and rivers dammed for industrial purposes. However, good progress is now being made as a result of aquaculture, natural restocking and the introduction of strict quotas both for leisure and industrial fishing. Stocks are now improving on both the Atlantic and Pacific coasts, and in the Great Lakes, particularly in the case of the white sturgeon.

Wisconsin is just one US state that is actively trying to restock its rivers with its native Great Lakes sturgeon (*A fulvescens*). And, since 1994 the state has accorded the Menimee tribe the legal right to some of the sturgeon. The Native Americans are permitted to kill sturgeon for their ceremonial spring feast, which was traditionally held to celebrate the end of the long winter months during which protein was scarce. The return of the migratory fish was believed to rejuvenate the tribesmen.

California currently has several sturgeon farms, the largest of which estimates that it will produce 10 tonnes of white sturgeon caviar by 2003. The state also exports fingerlings to Italy for its own breeding programme. However, the flavour of the eggs lacks consistency, and to date cannot match the quality of properly produced Caspian caviar. Michigan, Missouri and South Carolina are just three other states that are running restocking programmes to increase the sturgeon population in North America.

Below: A freshly caught sturgeon being taken to the shore based processing station as quickly and carefully as possible.

THE VARIETIES

*The largest Russian
Beluga sturgeon on record
was the length of eleven
men standing shoulder to
shoulder and was caught
in 1908 in Astrakhan.
It contained 450 kg,
or 990 lb of eggs.*

ALMAS

White caviar is something for élitists — very hard to acquire and therefore a curiosity.

ANTON MOSIMANN

"Golden caviar" was formerly reserved for the Emperors of Manchuria, the Tsars of Russia and even for the Vatican. In Iran it was kept exclusively for the Shah, and anyone caught selling or eating it had their right hand chopped off.

There are several theories among caviar experts as to what "golden caviar" actually is. It is generally thought to be either the eggs of an albino sturgeon or those of an Oscietre sturgeon over 60 years of age (whose eggs can be known to change to a light golden colour). Some importers grade these eggs as "Almas" caviar. In any case, it is extremely rare and there is a long waiting list for this product, even though it costs many thousands of dollars per kilo. Almas is packed to order in 50 g (2 oz) or 250 g (9 oz) gold tins, complete with a gold spoon, and is placed in a specially veneered wooden humidor. Sometimes in older Beluga and Oscietre sturgeon there is a pocket of pale eggs behind the gills of the fish, and these are also highly prized.

The flavour of albino eggs is incredibly light and delicate, while the flavour of pale Oscietre eggs from a mature fish is marvellously creamy and subtle. It has to be the ultimate caviar for the lover's seduction scene.

BELUGA

HUSO HUSO

Caspian fishermen dream of catching a great Beluga – it is tantamount to finding a diamond in the desert.

The Beluga is the biggest of all sturgeons (up to 6 m/20 ft in length) and is the only carnivore. It is so incredibly rare that barely more than 100 fish per year are now caught in the Caspian waters. The Beluga has been known to weigh 600 kg (1,323 lb) or more, but unfortunately, because of aggressive modern fishing methods such a size seems extremely unlikely these days. At the beginning of the twentieth century the Beluga accounted for 40 per cent of the sturgeon catch – today it is barely one per cent.

The Beluga is silvery-grey in colour and differs from other sturgeon in that it loses the bony scales along its length after it is a few months old. It has a big, short head with a pointed snout and a large mouth, which in a full-grown fish is up to 25 cm (10 in) wide. Two sets of barbels (rather like whiskers), which all sturgeon use to locate their food, are situated under its mouth. Up to 25 per cent of the Beluga's body weight may consist of eggs, although individual fish have been recorded carrying up to 50 per cent. The female does not mature until about 25 years of age and may not spawn every year. Like all sturgeon, Beluga can keep their eggs inside them for more than one season, if the conditions and temperature are not favourable for spawning.

Because of its immense size, the Beluga generally has the biggest eggs, which are the most highly prized for their large grain and fine skin. The egg colour varies from light grey to nearly black. The lightest grey is the most highly appreciated, although the taste, described by experts as "a faint flavour of the sea", should not be affected by the egg colour. Recent times have seen Beluga caviar double in price within a period of months.

SEVRUGA

Small, dark and distinctive, Sevruga is the choice of those who like their eggs full of taste and flavour.

The Sevruga is the smallest sturgeon caught commercially. It grows to a maximum of 1.5 m (5 ft) and rarely exceeds 25 kg (55 lb) in weight. It has a snub nose with a long snout and two sets of barbels, just above its small mouth. Like the Oscietre, the Sevruga is an omnivore and bottom-feeds on algae and small crustacea. It has very distinctive bony scales down its length, which resemble stars, and for this reason it is sometimes known as the star sturgeon. It has a striking backbone and mottled body, which may be deep blackish-brown, cinnamon-brown, ash-grey or nearly black. Sevruga are nearly always darker when living in the sea than they are in rivers.

The female Sevruga starts producing eggs at about 7 to 10 years old, earlier than other sturgeon, from which time 10–12 per cent of its body weight consists of eggs. The fish is at its prime when caught between 18 and 22 years of age, when its eggs are at their best.

Right: The tin in the centre of the picture contains Sevruga caviar.

The eggs are grey-black with a fine grain, small and have the strongest flavour of all sturgeon eggs. Among connoisseurs they are the most highly appreciated for their unique taste. Sevruga caviar is also the least expensive, mainly because Sevruga sturgeon are to be found in greater numbers.

OSCIETRE

ACIPENSER GUELDENSTAEDTI

The most intriguing fish, with more subtle nuances of flavour, size and colour in her egg than any other sturgeon.

The Oscietre is in some ways the most interesting sturgeon in that its eggs have the greatest variety in terms of size, flavour and colour. It is said that the taste of the eggs varies so much because the Oscietre is a bottom-feeder and takes on the flavour of whatever it is eating. If you were to open ten 1.8-kg (4-lb) tins of Oscietre caviar simultaneously, each one would smell, taste and look different, even if the fish had been caught at the same time and the eggs processed at the same fishing station.

The Oscietre grows up to 2 m (6½ ft) in length and can weigh up to 200 kg (440 lb), although the average mature fish grows to 1.5 m (5 ft) and weighs only 20–80 kg (44–176 lb). It has a short, thick head with a slightly pointed nose and a small mouth that protrudes like a small suction pipe to suck up algae, plants, small fish and other crustacea. The fish has bony scales down the length of its body, and its colour varies from dark grey to brown on the backbone, with a lighter-coloured stomach. It also has two sets of barbels above its mouth.

Oscietre can live for 60 to 80 years, and in the past some have been caught aged up to 120 years. They mature at 12 to 15 years of age. Those bred in warmer aquaculture conditions can mature earlier at 8 to 10 years. The eggs vary enormously in colour, from dark grey to dark brown and gold. Even in young fish the eggs are large in size and mostly of a dark golden shade. As the fish ages the roe fades to a light shade of amber and has a tremendously subtle flavour, described as "walnuts and cream".

FROM SHIP TO SHOP

The largest Iranian Beluga sturgeon was recorded in 1924. It was 6 m or 19½ ft long, 170 years old and contained about 375 kg or 827 lb of eggs.

THE CAVIAR
PROCESS

Caviar is not kosher – the sturgeon loses its scales as it ages. Some Jewish people do consider it appropriate to eat as the fish has scales before reaching maturity.

Fishing for sturgeon has been a proud tradition for generations. The key role is that of the master caviar processor, whose skill is essential to this delicate and valuable commodity. Although there are huge factory fishing vessels operating all year round in the Caspian, producing mainly pasteurized caviar, most sturgeon fishing remains essentially the same as in previous centuries. In Iran small boats are used, each with about four fishermen, who cast their nets by hand and handle the fish carefully, as the eggs must be taken from the fish as soon the boats reach the fishing stations.

The main fishing seasons are spring and autumn (although illegal fishing concerns based in other Caspian states take no heed of the seasons). When the fish are caught, they are taken straight to one of the fishing stations positioned close to the shore. In Iran, these are all owned and controlled by Shilat, the official state fishery. There is still an official Russian state fishery in Moscow, although its influence has greatly diminished in recent years.

Overleaf: The swelling to perfectly round eggs only takes place once they are packed inside the sealed tins.

At the fishing stations, the female sturgeon are placed on large slabs and stunned, then washed and scrubbed with fresh water. They are then cut open from tail to head, taking great care not to damage the eggs, which are removed together with their membrane. The spinal cord (*vesiga*) and swimbladder are also removed at this point. The rest of the fish is set aside for canning, smoking or freezing.

The roe is then handled by the caviar processor, who sorts the various varieties, grades them according to size and colour, and judges the condition of the whole roe in terms of its maturity. Next the eggs are rubbed gently through a mesh sieve large enough to allow them to pass through but leave the membrane behind. Then the eggs are washed in cold water to rinse off any remaining debris. This process is repeated until the master caviar processor is satisfied that they are clean.

The eggs are then transferred into vats in batches of not more than 5–15 kg (11–33 lb) at a time, and pure salt is shaken evenly over the egg surface. This process creates the unique flavour of caviar and the exact "magic formula" hinges on the judgement and skill of the expert caviar processor. He knows instinctively how much salt should be added and how long to stir the mixture to obtain the correct texture and consistency.

The skin of the sturgeon makes a very fine leather, resembling reptile skin – especially the skin of the Sevruga, with its distinctive star markings. In China they make brightly coloured coats and bags out of the skins.

Normally 2.5–3.5 per cent salt is added in Iran, and 3.5–4 per cent in Russia. The exact amount will depend on the eggs' quality, maturity and the actual salt content required. In Russia a small quantity of the mineral borax is often added with the salt as it is believed to sweeten and preserve the caviar. A small amount is permissible in Europe, but in the US and Japan borax is a banned substance. The caviar is then packed into 1.8 kg (4 lb) tins and the lids firmly sealed by a press that expels any surplus oils and salt (this does not damage the eggs). A wide rubber band is placed around the tins, and the eggs swell up until they are perfectly round. The tins are then wiped clean and labelled. In Iran Shilat marks all its tins with a special code identifying the fishing station that processed the sturgeon, the type of fish, the grade of the eggs, date of catch, the weight of roe per fish and the number of tins in each batch.

Overleaf: The roe is very carefully washed and removed from the fish (in this case, Oscietre).

The whole caviar process should take less than 20 minutes to ensure maximum freshness and to ensure exposure to the air is kept to a minimum. Naturally, the utmost care is taken to keep the conditions in the factory absolutely sterile to eliminate any risk of bacterial contamination. Random checks to monitor the quality are carried out by major customers who pierce a needle through the tin into the eggs, remove a little oil then examine it carefully.

Above: Before the salt is added the eggs are passed several times through a wide-mesh sieve to remove the membrane.

The tins of caviar are placed into linen bags three at a time. These are tightly sewn up and sealed with a lead seal. Four of the bags are then carefully packed into specially fitted plywood boxes weighing around 20 kg (44 lb) each. The boxes are kept at a constant temperature of around -2°C (28°F), until ready for export under refrigeration. The salt in the caviar ensures it will not freeze even at such a low temperature.

Most large importers of caviar receive their stock in this form and will either sell on the original tins or alternatively repackage the caviar at the required weight and use their own labelling. Every tin bought from a reputable vendor should at least have a sell-by date on it and some also give the date of catch.

This page: Tins are loosely filled and the lids pressed firmly down. This does not damage the eggs. A wide rubber band is used to seal the tins after special identification marks are stamped on each tin.

ENJOYING CAVIAR

Caviar comes from the
virgin sturgeon
Virgin sturgeon's one
fine dish
Virgin sturgeon needs
no urgin'
That's why caviar is
my dish.

ANON

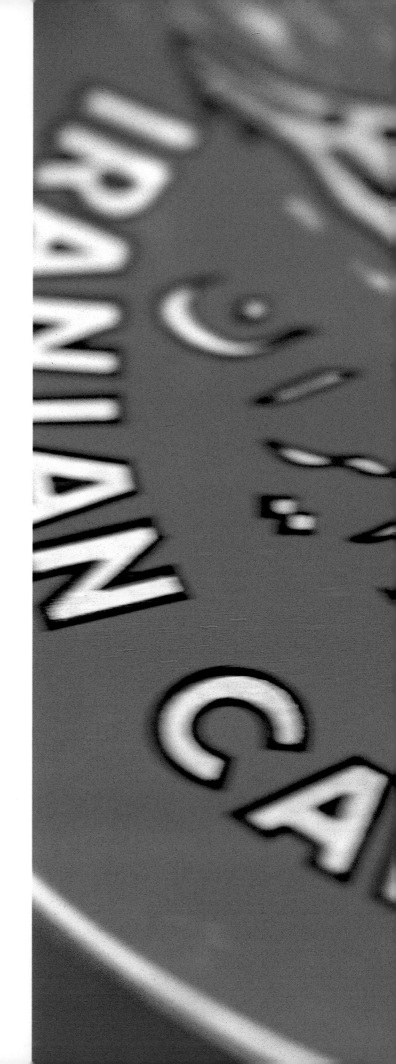

BUYING AND SERVING

When you decide to embark on buying caviar there are several important factors to bear in mind. Like any good food item, it should have been stored properly before you acquired it and must be as fresh as possible.

The majority of established retailers now pack their caviar by vacuum-seal. A good vendor will guarantee the quality with clear labelling, often adding extra seals. Otherwise, the caviar may have been incorrectly packed or, worse, it may have been replaced with inferior caviar. Fishing stations – and some retailers - use wide rubber bands to seal the tins, but there should not be any difference in the quality however they are sealed. Caviar is also sold in glass jars of varying sizes. The vast factory fishing ships process, grade and immediately pack their caviar with screw- or grip-top lids; then they generally pasteurize it. Caviar in glass jars can seem deceptively large as the glass can magnify the eggs. If the quality is high, the eggs should follow the jar round when it is turned slowly. It is best to avoid caviar packed in sealed tins unless you are confident of their origin.

To taste caviar, put a gold or otherwise non-metallic spoon vertically into the tin or jar, then place a little caviar on the back of your hand in the V between your thumb and first finger (or your partner's!). Eat it from the skin, rolling the eggs in your mouth, then gently popping them to release their full flavour. Lastly, rub the skin of your hand: there should be no residual odour.

Caviar's greatest enemies are air and heat, so tins should always be full. Keep caviar in the refrigerator and carefully note its sell-by date. Pasteurized caviar is the only exception to this and may be kept at room temperature for several months. If you do keep tins in a refrigerator for a few weeks, it is quite a good idea to turn them from time to time, as this ensures that the natural oils stay well distributed among the eggs.

Once you open a tin of caviar, always return any leftover eggs to the refrigerator as soon as possible, transferring them from the tin to a glass jar covered with clingfilm. Unopened caviar can be kept in a domestic refrigerator for two to three months at around 3°C (37°F). An industrial refrigerator can keep caviar for up to a year at -3°C to -5°C (26–22°F), depending on the salt content. Never freeze caviar, as the eggs will normally break down on defrosting.

Left: The classic way of serving caviar – on a bed of ice with a horn spoon.

Right: A simple breakfast on the shores of the Caspian Sea – freshly processed caviar with crusty bread.

Any caviar that has been opened should be treated as you would any fresh fish – that is, eaten within two or three days. If the eggs have a tart, acid or fishy smell, return them to the retailer, who, if he is reputable, will change them. If there is anything other than eggs and oil in your tin (such as bits of membrane, specks of blood or white crystals around the eggs), return it to the vendor immediately. This means that the roe was not properly cleaned when processed or, in the case of crystals, is old and the salt has separated. This is sometimes the case with black-market caviar bought on street corners. Do not eat it – it can be extremely dangerous to your health.

Very occasionally people are allergic to caviar. If you do have an allergic reaction, seek immediate medical advice and treat it the same way as oyster poisoning. Do not eat caviar again, as it will have a cumulative effect and your next reaction will be worse.

PRESENTATION

If you are lucky enough to have a caviar server made either of glass or shell, arrange the tin or jar within it, or turn the eggs out into the serving dish. Take the tin out of the refrigerator about half an hour before serving, but do not open it until you are ready to serve the caviar. Otherwise, crush some ice in a suitably sized bowl and embed the tin or jar of caviar on top.

Left: The accepted professional method of savouring and tasting caviar.

Right: Champagne is always a suitably luxurious accompaniment to caviar.

Never use a metal spoon (unless it is gold), as this will oxidize the caviar and alter its flavour. If you do not have a special caviar spoon, then use a plastic one, because it will not affect the flavour of the caviar or take on any odour. Always put the spoon vertically into the eggs to avoid crushing them. Lemon also oxidizes caviar, so avoid squeezing it over the eggs unless they have been pressed or pasteurized.

WHAT TO DRINK

The Russian national spirit, vodka, is the perfect partner for caviar. A colourless and naturally unflavoured spirit, it can be distilled from sources such as potatoes, rye and barley, but was originally made principally from wheat. Even in the 16th century various roots, herbs and fruits were added to vodka to enhance it. It is now readily available in a bewildering range of flavours. Since the Russians are the largest consumers of caviar and vodka is their national drink, it seems inevitable that they have come to be eaten and drunk together, whether for special occasions or every day.

Vodka should always be served icy cold. If you keep good-quality vodka in your freezer it will not actually freeze, due to its high alcohol content (35–80 per cent), but has the consistency syrup when poured. However, because of their lower alcohol content, some cheaper vodkas have been known to freeze in the bottle.

A classic caviar cocktail is made by pouring ice-cold vodka into a chilled glass, then dropping a spoonful of caviar through the glacial liquid to rest on the bowl of the glass. As you reach the end of your drink the simplicity of the vodka cuts through and offsets the slightly salty texture of the caviar.

If you are making a recipe that combines shellfish with caviar, it is important to remember that many people find this combination indigestible with vodka or other spirits. In this situation you may be wise to stick to wine or Champagne.

White wines and Champagne are in some ways an easier option in any case. If you are using a strong-flavoured caviar and gutsy ingredients, such as onions, then serve a NV Champagne, or the taste of the dish will completely overwhelm it. Elegant, crisp dry white wines such as Sancerre and other good Sauvignon Blancs are delicious served with caviar, as are unoaked or lightly oaked Chardonnays such as Chablis. Some of the New World Chardonnays are good, but it is wise to avoid those that are heavy and oaky, as they tend to be too rich and will overwhelm the caviar.

We have offered some suggestions alongside our recipes, based on personal taste and experience, but our preferences may not necessarily accord with yours, and you should not be afraid to experiment for yourself. But, as caviar is normally served as an event, to seduce, to impress or just because you like it, it is important to accompany it with the drink of your choice.

CANAPES

CAVIAR AND SMOKED SALMON CHEQUERBOARD

This is a classic canapé, that is often served in top hotels. Beluga is the best variety to use, but, depending on the depth of your pocket, it can also be made with Oscietre or Sevruga. For a sensational impact you could use Beluga and Almas caviar instead of smoked salmon to contrast with it.

6 slices thin white sandwich loaf
50 g (2 oz) butter
125 g (4½ oz) Beluga caviar
225 g (8 oz) sliced smoked salmon

1 Lightly toast six or more slices of thin white bread (preferably a square loaf, if you can find one) and spread thinly with butter.

2 Take half the slices and spread them with caviar. Cover the other slices with the smoked salmon. Trim off the crusts and, using a sharp knife, cut all the slices into equal-sized squares or diamonds.

3 Place side by side, alternating the caviar and the smoked salmon, so that you end up with a chequerboard appearance. Serve immediately.

Makes about 54

SERVE WITH *NV Champagne or vodka.*

SLICED LOBSTER TAIL AND CAVIAR ON CROUTONS

You can use ordinary toast instead of croûtons if you prefer, but it is tastier with the seasoned croûtons in the recipe.

light oil for frying
½ chicken stockcube
4 slices white bread
1 lobster tail
50 g (2 oz) Sevruga caviar

1 Heat the oil in a large frying pan. Crumble the stockcube into the oil, then fry the bread until it turns an even, gold colour. Drain well on kitchen paper.

2 Using a small round cutter, cut out circles of fried bread. Slice the lobster tail vertically into medallions and place one on top of each croûton. Top with caviar.

Makes 12

SERVE WITH *NV Rosé Champagne or good white burgundy (ie Côte de Beaune Premiers or Grands Crus).*

JERSEY ROYALS WITH CAVIAR

You will find that these get eaten faster than you can make them!

*20 very small new potatoes
(preferably Jersey Royals)
50 g (2 oz) caviar*

1 Simply scrub and boil the new potatoes until they are cooked. Cut them in half lengthways, slicing a bit off the bottoms, so that they do not fall over. Then simply top with the caviar of your choice.

Makes 40

SERVE WITH *NV Brut or Rosé Champagne.*

BABY NEW POTATOES WITH SMOKED HADDOCK AND CAVIAR FILLING

This recipe is delicately flavoured and tasty, and is ideal for a drinks party. You could substitute salmon eggs for the caviar, if you wish. It can also be adapted to make a main course, using larger potatoes.

*20 baby new potatoes
100 g (3½ oz) smoked haddock fillet
300 ml (10 fl oz) milk
freshly ground black pepper
100 ml (3½ fl oz) sour cream
1 tsp lemon juice
1 tbsp parsley, freshly chopped
100 g (3½ oz) Sevruga caviar*

1 Boil the potatoes until tender, then drain and cool. In a saucepan, bring the smoked haddock and milk to simmering point. Cook for 5 minutes. Drain the fish and flake into a bowl.

2 Cut the potatoes in half. Using a sharp teaspoon, carefully scoop out the flesh, then mash it in a bowl. Add quarter of the mashed potato to the haddock, season with pepper and mix well. Using a fork, carefully blend in the sour cream, lemon juice and parsley and half the caviar. Spoon the mixture into the potato shells. Garnish with the remaining caviar.

Makes 40

SERVE WITH *NV Champagne or fine white Bordeaux (ie Graves or Péssac-Léognan).*

FRIED QUAIL EGGS ON TOAST, TOPPED WITH CAVIAR

A subtle luxury!

3 slices thin white sandwich loaf
12 fresh quail eggs
50 g (2 oz) butter
freshly ground black pepper
30–50 g (1–2 oz) Oscietre caviar

1 Lightly toast the bread and cut it into 12 rounds, using a cutter with a diameter of about 4 cm (1½ in). Keep warm in the oven on a wire rack.

2 Using a large, sharp knife, break all the quail eggs into a bowl keeping the yolks intact (this can be difficult, as the membrane is rather thick). Heat the butter in a large saucepan, then carefully tip all the eggs and the black pepper into the pan. Using a spatula, make sure that the eggs are evenly spread around the base. Put the lid on the pan and fry for a couple of minutes, frequently checking them until they are cooked. Remove from the heat and, using the cutter, cut out each fried egg.

3 Place the rounds of toast on a serving dish and place a quail egg on each one, topping it with ½ tsp of caviar.

Makes 12

SERVE WITH *vintage Champagne, top Chablis (Grand Cru) or white Bordeaux (ie Graves or Péssac-Léognan).*

ROASTED POTATO SKINS WITH SOUR CREAM AND CAVIAR

Keep the potato centres from this recipe for another dish – if you have any sour cream and shallots left over, you can mash them all together, make them into patties and fry them until golden brown.

4 large baking potatoes
150 ml (5 fl oz) oil for deep-frying
200 ml (7 fl oz) sour cream
salt and white pepper
100 g (3½ oz) Oscietre caviar
2–3 shallots, finely chopped

1 Preheat the oven to 180°C (350°F/Gas Mark 4). Wash and dry the potatoes, then prick them several times with a fork. Bake in the oven for approximately 1¼ hours.

2 Slice the potatoes open and scoop out as much flesh as possible with a spoon. Cut the skins into strips about 2.5 cm (1 in) wide by 7.5 cm (3 in) long. In a large saucepan heat the oil and, when bubbling, drop in the potato strips and fry until they turn crisp and golden brown. Remove with a slotted spoon and drain well upside-down on several sheets of kitchen paper.

3 Arrange the potato strips on a serving dish, smear with sour cream, then sprinkle with salt and pepper. Top each with caviar and sprinkle with finely chopped shallots.

Makes about 20

SERVE WITH *vodka.*

MINI BAKED POTATOES
WITH CAVIAR

This is a delicious canapé for a special occasion and seems to go perfectly with a glass of Champagne and a real fire on a cold winter's night. It also works well accompanying a plate of smoked salmon or lightly seasoned and buttered, pan-fried salmon steaks. Serve with some peas or mangetout.

12 mature potatoes
(the smallest you can find)
175 ml (6 fl oz) sour cream
2 tbsp chives, finely chopped
freshly ground black pepper
juice of 1 onion
1 tsp lemon juice (optional)
150 ml (5 fl oz) oil for deep-frying
30 g (1 oz) butter
100 g (3½ oz) Oscietre caviar

1 Preheat the oven to 200°C (400°F/Gas Mark 6). Scrub and dry the potatoes. Prick each with a skewer, then place on a shallow baking dish and cook in the oven for about 40 minutes.

2 Mix together the sour cream, chives, a generous grinding of pepper and the onion juice, plus the lemon juice (if desired). Set the mixture aside.

3 Remove the potatoes from the oven and cut in half lengthways. Carefully scoop out the flesh, keeping the skins complete, but slicing a little off the bottoms, so that the potatoes will sit upright. Lightly mash the soft potato, set aside and keep warm.

4 In a large saucepan heat the oil and, when bubbling, drop in the potato skins and fry until they turn crisp and golden brown. Remove with a slotted spoon and drain well upside-down on several sheets of kitchen paper.

5 Using a large fork, whip the mashed potatoes with the butter and the sour cream, chive, onion and lemon-juice mixture. Put a large teaspoonful into each potato skin and top with ½ tsp of caviar. Serve immediately or the skins may turn soggy.

Makes 24

SERVE WITH *vintage Champagne, Chablis, white Bordeaux (ie Graves or Péssac-Léognan) or vodka.*

MINI PIZZAS TOPPED WITH CAVIAR

These make a sophisticated but simple, bite-sized snack, that
even Italians should be happy to hand round at a party.

Pizza bases
1½ tsp dried yeast or 10 g (¼ oz) fresh yeast
250 ml (8 fl oz) luke-warm water
375 g (12 oz) strong plain flour
salt and freshly ground black pepper
*2 tbsp virgin olive oil, plus a little extra
to oil the bowl*

Topping
100 ml (3½ fl oz) crème fraîche
50 g (2 oz) Sevruga or Oscietre caviar
200 g (7 oz) smoked salmon
1 tbsp dill, roughly snipped

1 Preheat the oven to 230°C (450°F/Gas Mark 8), and insert a lightly oiled baking pan. Sprinkle the yeast over 2 tbsp of the warm water in a small bowl; allow to stand for about 5 minutes until dissolved. Sift the flour with 1 tsp of salt and ½ tsp of pepper. Make a well in the centre and add the yeast mixture, the oil and the remaining water. Combine all the ingredients together and work into a dough; keep kneading the dough until it is smooth and elastic, which should take about 8 minutes.

2 Lightly oil a large bowl. Put the dough in the bowl, cover with a damp cloth or clingfilm and allow to rise in a warm place for about 1 hour, until doubled in size (or you can leave the dough to rise overnight in the refrigerator).

3 Pull off a small amount of dough and roll into a ball about 2 cm (¾ in) in diameter. You will need a well-floured board as this dough is rather sticky. Press it into a flat pizza shape, about 5 cm (2 in) across. Place the "pizzas" on a floured baking sheet, until you have filled it with the rounds. Then pull out the hot baking sheet from the oven and quickly transfer the pizzas onto it. Put into the oven immediately and cook for 8–10 minutes until crisp.

4 Spread the cooked pizzas with crème fraîche then place a small piece of smoked salmon on one half of each one. Place a small spoonful of caviar on the other half and garnish with dill.

Makes about 20 depending on the desired size

SERVE WITH *NV Champagne, Sancerre/Pouilly-Fumé, Mosel Riesling Kabinett or Pinot Bianco.*

QUAIL EGGS WITH CAVIAR

Quail eggs make marvellous bite-sized canapés and the delicate flavour complements the caviar perfectly. Here is a classic excuse for using the best caviar you can obtain, but if you are preparing a plateful of the eggs, alternate the caviar with some salmon or trout eggs to give a good colour contrast.

12 fresh quail eggs
(you can buy these pre-cooked and peeled, but they taste better if you have time to cook them yourself)
30 g (1 oz) caviar

1 Drop the quail eggs into a saucepan of hot water. Bring rapidly to the boil for 2 minutes. Drain and place the eggs in a bowl of cold water. Crack each egg all over and, using the end of a teaspoon, carefully peel off the shell.

2 Cut each egg in half lengthways and place on a plate. Top with a few grains of caviar or salmon roe. Simple and quite delicious!

Makes 24

SERVE WITH *vintage Champagne, Chablis or white Bordeaux (ie Graves or Péssac-Léognan).*

HARD-BOILED HEN'S EGGS TOPPED WITH CAVIAR

Sevruga caviar is good to use in this recipe, as its stronger taste complements the other ingredients. It is also fun and makes for a colourful combination to top some of the eggs with salmon or trout eggs.

4 fresh hen's eggs
30–50 g (1–2 oz) Sevruga caviar

Crème fraîche and onion filling
50 g (2 oz) crème fraîche
½ red onion, finely chopped (or chives, if you consider onion too strong for canapés)
1 tsp lemon juice
salt and freshly ground black pepper

Shrimp filling
50 g (2 oz) peeled shrimps, finely chopped
1 tbsp dill, chopped
1–2 tbsp mayonnaise
1 tsp lemon juice
salt and freshly ground white pepper

1 Boil the eggs for 8 minutes. Plunge them into cold water for a couple of minutes, then peel them and cut in half lengthways with a sharp knife. Retain the white part. Mash the yolks, then combine with one of the fillings, seasoning to taste.

2 Using a teaspoon, carefully stuff the white part of the eggs with your chosen filling, flattening off the tops. Just before serving, decorate with the caviar.

Makes 8

SERVE WITH *NV Rosé Champagne.*

CHOUX PUFFS FILLED WITH CAVIAR

There are many delicious fillings that you could add to these
mouth-watering choux puffs.

Choux puffs
80 g (3 oz) plain flour
¼ tsp salt
pinch of white pepper
40 g (1½ oz) cold butter, diced
150 ml (5 fl oz) cold water
3 egg yolks
2 egg whites, beaten

Crème fraîche and chive filling
250 ml (8 fl oz) crème fraîche or
cottage cheese
2 tbsp chives, finely chopped

1 tbsp red onion, finely chopped
¼ tsp freshly ground black pepper
2 tsp lemon juice
50 g (2 oz) Sevruga caviar

Crabmeat filling
150 ml (5 fl oz)
100 g (4 oz) shredded crabmeat
1 tbsp parsley, finely chopped
2 tsp lemon juice
50 g (2 oz) Sevruga caviar

1 Preheat the oven to 220°C (425°F/Gas Mark 7). Sift the flour, salt and white pepper into a bowl.

2 Add the diced butter and water to a heavy, medium-sized saucepan. Bring slowly to the boil so that the butter melts completely. Remove from the heat and quickly add all the flour at once, beating until smooth. On a low heat, continue to beat the mixture for about 2 minutes, until it separates cleanly from the sides of the pan into a ball around the spoon.

3 Remove the pan from the heat and beat in two of the egg yolks. Then, little by little, add the egg whites until the mixture becomes smooth and shiny.

4 Lightly grease two baking sheets and, using a teaspoon make balls of choux paste 2.5 cm (1 in) in diameter, placing them 1 cm (½ in) apart on the baking sheet. Beat the third egg yolk and glaze each puff using a pastry brush, taking care not to let the yolk drip onto the baking sheet, as this will stop your puffs rising

evenly. Cook for 10 minutes, then reduce the heat to 160°C (325°F/Gas Mark 3). Bake for another 15 minutes, or until the choux puffs are crisp, light and a rich golden colour.

5 Remove the puffs from the oven and then slit the sides with a sharp knife to allow the steam to escape to prevent them going soggy. Scrape out any uncooked pastry in the centre. Cool on a wire rack and store in an airtight container.

6 Combine your filling ingredients except for the caviar in a bowl. Cut the puffs in half and fill one side with a teaspoonful of the mixture. On the other side put a teaspoonful of caviar. Place the sides back together, at an angle so that the caviar shows. Alternatively, you could combine salmon caviar with the crabmeat.

Makes about 20

SERVE WITH NV Champagne, Chablis, Sancerre/Pouilly-Fumé or Mosel Riesling Kabinett.

MINI STEAK TARTARE AND CAVIAR

Many people have given us variations of this classic recipe and this is our
favourite. Make sure that you get your beef from a good source and that both
it and the eggs are very fresh.

*500 g (1¼ lb) fresh fillet of beef
(preferably organic)
2 free-range egg yolks
2½ tbsp onion, minced
2 tbsp capers, minced
4 tbsp parsley, finely chopped
3 anchovy fillets, finely chopped
pinch of paprika
1 tsp Tabasco sauce*

*2 tsp Worcestershire sauce
salt and freshly ground black pepper
1 tsp brandy
4 slices white sandwich loaf
40 g (1½ oz) butter
4 quail eggs
50 g (2 oz) Beluga caviar
salad leaves to garnish*

1 Mince the beef finely, then place in a large
mixing bowl. Combine the egg yolks, onion,
capers, parsley and anchovies thoroughly with
the fillet. Add the other seasonings and brandy.

2 Using a cutter, cut out 5 cm (2 in) rounds
from the bread slices and fry in half the butter.
Drain on kitchen paper.

3 Divide the beef tartare into eight equal
portions and fashion into mini-beefburgers, to
fit onto the fried bread rounds.

4 In the remaining butter, fry the quail
eggs, then top four of the beefburgers with
caviar and four with a quail egg. Garnish with
baby salad leaves.

5 You can also serve the beef tartare mixture
on fingers of toast, topped with Beluga – this
was a favourite late-night snack in a famous
London nightclub. Another speciality is to roll
the beef tartare into bite-sized balls, flattening
them a little. Cut them in half crossways with
a sharp knife, then, using a teaspoon, indent
the centres of each half and fill with caviar.
Stick the halves back together again, enclosing
the caviar in the centre. Put a little oil into a
pan over a high heat and sear each side of the
thick mini-beefburgers, so that the top and
bottom are both well browned, but the centre
remains raw.

Serves 4

SERVE WITH *Vintage Rosé Champagne or young
red low in tannin (ie Chinon Jeunes Vignes,
Cru Beaujolais).*

VOL-AU-VENT FISH FILLED WITH CAVIAR

These can be made the previous day and reheated just before serving. If you can't find a cutter in the shape of a fish, cut out your own fish shapes, using a very sharp knife.

30 g (1 oz) flour for rolling out pastry
225 g (8 oz) puff pastry
1 egg yolk
1 tbsp milk
50 g (2 oz) Oscietre caviar

1 Preheat the oven to 220°C (425°F/Gas Mark 7). On a lightly floured board, roll out the pastry evenly to about 5 mm (¼ in) thick. Cut out simple fish shapes about 8 cm (3 in) long and 5 cm (2 in) wide on the body. Make an oval indent with a knife in the middle of the fish – this will be cut out later to make a lid.

2 Line a baking dish with baking parchment and place the pastry fish on it, leaving 2 cm (¾ in) between each one. Place in the refrigerator for 20 minutes to rest.

3 Beat the egg yolk and milk together, then carefully paint the top of the fish with it, taking care that the mixture does not drip down the sides. Bake for 10–12 minutes until well risen and golden brown. Remove from the oven and, using a sharp knife, carefully cut out the lids and some of the insides. Place on a wire rack and keep warm.

4 Fill each fish with ½ tsp of caviar and arrange on a plate, topping them with the lids (or discard these if you prefer).

Makes about 25

SERVE WITH NV Champagne, Sancerre/Pouilly-Fumé or Chablis.

SMOKED SALMON MONEY BAGS FILLED WITH CAVIAR

These are a bit fiddly to make, but look very attractive and are well worth the effort.

275 g (10 oz) large slices
of smoked salmon
150 ml (5 fl oz) crème fraîche
50 g (2 oz) Oscietre caviar
bunch of chives

1 Using a sharp knife, cut the smoked salmon into roughly 8 cm (3 in) squares. Place ½ tsp of crème fraîche and ½ tsp of caviar in the centre of each square. Gather up into a bag and tie around the neck with two chives.

Makes about 10

SERVE WITH NV Rosé Champagne, Chablis, Sancerre/Pouilly-Fumé or Mosel Riesling Kabinett.

CAVIAR AND CHIPS

30 g (1 oz) Sevruga caviar
450 g (1 lb) potatoes
oil for deep frying
30 g (1 oz) crème fraîche (optional)

1 Wash and peel the potatoes; cut into chunky chip-sized rectangles. Rinse thoroughly in cold water.

2 Bring a saucepan of salted water to the boil and cook the potatoes for 6-7 minutes. They should still be hard. Drain and dry well on kitchen paper.

3 In a deep fryer with a wire basket, heat the oil until it tries to bubble. Put the chips in a wire basket into the oil very carefully to avoid the oil spitting and cook for about 5 minutes until they turn light gold. Tip the chips out of the basket onto several layers of kitchen paper. When you wish to serve them, reheat the oil and return them to the wire basket and fry them a second time for about 2 minutes or until golden and crisp. Drain onto kitchen paper, shaking well to absorb any excess oil.

4 Sit the chips up and dab a teaspoon of crème fraîche (optional) and a teaspoon of caviar on top of each.

Serves 4

***SERVE WITH** NV Champagne, Chablis or vodka*

POACHED OYSTERS WITH CHAMPAGNE SAUCE AND CAVIAR

The ultimate aphrodisiac must be raw oysters with caviar, but for those of you who want added luxury, these are poached with a Champagne sauce.

12 fresh oysters in their shells
300 ml (10 fl oz) fish stock
300 ml (10 fl oz) Champagne
2 tbsp double cream
50 g (2 oz) diced butter
salt and pepper to taste
125 g (4 oz) Oscietre or Beluga caviar

1 Wash the oysters and open them with a short sharp knife over a bowl, retaining the liquid from the shells. Cut the muscle and remove oysters, stand in a sieve over the bowl. Keep the shells apart and wash them thoroughly.

Champagne Sauce

1 In a saucepan, bring the oyster juice, fish stock, Champagne and seasoning briskly to the boil and reduce to 300ml/10fl oz. Stir in two tablespoons of double cream until boiling, then add the oysters for one minute. Remove the oysters with a slotted spoon and keep warm.

2 Strain, return to saucepan and just return to boil. Remove sauce from heat, whisk in diced butter until smooth and then add a glass of Champagne and whisk again to lighten sauce.

3 On a warm serving dish, spread a generous layer of rock salt. Place half the shells onto it and place an oyster in each; spoon on the sauce and top each oyster with a teaspoon of caviar.

Serves 4

***SERVE WITH** your favourite Champagne*

POOR MAN'S DIP

This dip looks attractive and is very tasty, if you cannot stretch to the real thing. And if you add 2–3 tbsp of crème fraîche to the ingredients, you have a good sauce for a cold fish dish.

150 g (6 oz) mayonnaise
2–3 tsp lemon juice
2 tbsp herbs (basil, tarragon or dill),
finely chopped
1–2 tsp Dijon mustard
salt and black pepper
100 g (3½ oz) lumpfish roe (black or red)

1 Mix all the ingredients together, adding the roe at the last moment, just before serving.

SEVRUGA AND CHIVE DIP

This dip also makes a delicious filling for a baked potato.

175 ml (6 fl oz) fromage frais
85 ml (3 fl oz) sour cream
1 tsp onion, grated
1 tbsp chives, finely chopped
freshly ground black pepper
50 g (2 oz) Sevruga caviar

1 At room temperature, combine the fromage frais and sour cream. Stir in the onion, chives and pepper to taste. Put in the refrigerator.

2 Just before serving, carefully fold in the caviar, leaving ½ tsp with which to decorate the dip.

AVOCADO AND CAVIAR DIP

This delicious dip can be served either in individual portions as a starter or mounded in the centre of a large dish, surrounded with diamonds of crisp white toast.

3 ripe avocados
juice of ½ lemon
1 small white onion, finely chopped
1 tbsp crème fraîche
1 clove garlic (optional)
½ tsp mild paprika
salt and black pepper
30 g (1 oz) Sevruga caviar

1 Carefully cut the avocados in half lengthways and remove the stones. Spoon out the flesh into a food processor or blender, then add the lemon juice and onion. Blend until smooth, then stir in the crème fraîche, garlic, paprika, and salt and pepper to taste.

2 Turn the dip into a dish, cover with clingfilm and chill for at least 1 hour. Just before serving, place the caviar on the top.

All dips serve 4

SERVE DIPS WITH with NV Champagne, Chablis or Sancerre/Pouilly-Fumé.

CRAB AND CAVIAR IN CREPE TARTLETS

For an exquisitely fishy starter or snack try these tartlets. Alternatively, double
the quantities for an excellent lunch dish.

Crêpes
75 g (3 oz) plain flour
2 eggs, lightly beaten
2 tsp oil
120 ml (4 fl oz) milk
1 tbsp chives, finely chopped

Filling
30 g (1 oz) butter
½ onion, finely chopped
50 g (2 oz) plain flour
120 ml (4 fl oz) milk
100 g (3½ oz) fresh crabmeat
50 g (2 oz) Sevruga or Oscietre caviar

1 Preheat the oven to 200°C (400° F/Gas Mark 6). Sift the flour into a bowl. Gradually stir in the beaten eggs, then the oil, milk and chives and beat to a smooth batter. Cover and let stand in the refrigerator for at least ½ hour.

2 Lightly grease and heat a heavy-based pan. Pour 2–3 tbsp of batter into the pan and cook until golden brown, turning and repeating for the other side. Remove the crêpe from the pan and set aside; repeat with the rest of the batter mixture.

3 Using a cutter, cut out rounds from the crêpes, large enough to fit 10 cm (4 in) tartlet pans (the non-stick ones for mini-tarts are best for this). Line the tartlet pans with the crêpe rounds and bake for about 10 minutes, then remove from the pans and cool on a wire rack.

4 To make the filling, heat the butter in a saucepan. Add the onion and cook until soft. Stir in the flour, cooking for 1 minute. Remove from the heat, gradually stirring in the milk and crabmeat. Return to the heat and stir until the sauce boils and thickens. Allow to cool. Just before serving, spoon the crab mixture into the crêpe cups and top with caviar.

Makes 12

SERVE WITH *vintage Champagne, top white burgundy (ie Côtes de Beaune Premiers or Grands Crus), white Bordeaux (ie Graves or Pessac-Léognan) or Mosel Riesling Kabinett.*

SOUPS AND STARTERS

AVOCADO SOUP WITH SALMON AND CAVIAR

This pale green soup with its pink salmon strips is a marvellously colourful dish.
It makes a luxurious and impressive starter for a dinner party.

200 g (8 oz) fresh salmon fillet
salt and freshly ground black pepper
400 ml (14 fl oz) fish stock
or clear chicken stock
1 ripe avocado
1 tsp lemon juice
1 small glass of white wine
50 ml (2 fl oz) crème fraîche
or plain yoghurt
30 g (1 oz) Sevruga caviar

1 Cut the salmon fillet into thin strips
(a pair of sharp kitchen scissors is very
helpful here). Generously grind black
pepper over it and a little salt, and set aside.
Heat the stock in a large saucepan and
keep warm.

2 Halve the avocado and remove the stone.
Scoop out the flesh with a spoon, sprinkle it
with lemon juice, then combine in a blender or
food processor until smooth. Add it to the
saucepan of stock with the white wine, salt and
pepper, then whisk together until just
simmering. Remove from the heat and whisk
again vigorously.

3 Pour into heated soup bowls. Add some
salmon strips, with 1 tbsp of crème fraîche or
yoghurt, to each portion. Top with a
teaspoonful of caviar and serve immediately.
You can also add some vodka to give extra
flavour to the soup.

Serves 4

*SERVE WITH vodka, fino sherry or sercial
Madeira.*

TEMPURA OF AUBERGINE AND COURGETTE WITH CAVIAR

The flavour of the tempura and the fresh, deep-fried vegetables goes perfectly with caviar. This was a recipe that we tried with certain reservations, but found easy and delicious.

1 slim aubergine
salt
1 medium courgette
light oil for deep-frying (sunflower or vegetable)
½ red onion, finely chopped
100 g (4 oz) Oscietre or Beluga caviar
100 ml (3½ fl oz) crème fraîche

Batter
150 ml (5 fl oz) cold water
100 g (4 oz) plain flour
salt and freshly ground black pepper

1 Cut the aubergine into thin slices. Sprinkle salt on both sides and leave for ½ hour. Rinse well, then drain on kitchen paper. Peel and slice the courgette.

2 To make the batter, mix together the water, flour and a pinch of salt and pepper in a pudding bowl. The batter should be thick enough to stick to the vegetable slices, but not too thick.

3 Heat 50 ml (2 fl oz) of oil in a frying pan. Dip the slices of aubergine and courgette into the batter and fry immediately, until lightly golden on both sides (it is easy to burn these, so watch them carefully). Remove with a slotted spoon, drain well on kitchen paper and keep warm.

You may need to do two or three batches, depending on the size of your frying pan.

4 Taking four warm plates, arrange an equal number of fried aubergine and courgette slices around the edges. Sprinkle with a little chopped onion and top each with crème fraîche and a small teaspoonful of caviar.

Serves 4

SERVE WITH *Sancerre/Pouilly-Fumé, New Zealand Sauvignon or Clare Valley Riesling.*

WATERCRESS CAPPUCCINO WITH CAVIAR

You can serve this frothy, delicately flavoured soup in large, heated coffee cups to extend the cappuccino theme, that has become fashionable in many restaurants. This soup is light and has very few calories.

1 medium-sized leek, rinsed and finely chopped
2 tbsp olive oil
1 medium potato, peeled and finely chopped
600 ml (1 pt) vegetable stock
100 g (3½ oz) fresh watercress leaves (discard the stalks)
250 ml (8 fl oz) low-fat plain yoghurt
salt and freshly ground black pepper
50 g (2 oz) Sevruga caviar

1 In a medium-sized saucepan gently fry the leek in the oil until soft but not coloured. Add the potato and stir well. Pour over the vegetable stock and bring to the boil, then cover the pan and simmer for 15 minutes, or until the potato is tender. Add the watercress leaves and immediately remove the pan from the heat.

2 Spoon the mixture into a blender or food processor and process to a purée. Return to the pan and add the plain yoghurt and seasoning. Reheat the soup gently over a low heat. For the frothy finish, use a hand-held blender and whizz the soup until foamy. Serve warm with a spoonful of caviar on top.

Serves 4

SERVE WITH *vodka, top quality Sauvignon Blanc or Riesling.*

CREAM OF LEEK AND CAVIAR SOUP GRATINEE

This soup is fun and really different, with its grilled topping of whipped cream and caviar garnish.

30 g (1 oz) unsalted butter
500 g (1¼ lb) leeks (white part only), thinly sliced
salt
250 g (9 oz) potatoes, thinly sliced
1 litre (1¾ pt) clear chicken stock
300 ml (10 fl oz) whipping cream
freshly ground black pepper
50 g (2 oz) Sevruga caviar
1 tbsp parsley, finely chopped

1 Melt the butter in a large saucepan over a low heat. Add the leeks with a pinch of salt and cook slowly for about 10 minutes, or until the leeks are soft but not coloured. Add the potato and cook for another 3 minutes, then pour in the stock. Bring to the boil and simmer for 20 minutes. Add 175 ml (6 fl oz) of the cream and cook for another 10 minutes. Using a blender, purée the soup until smooth. Season with salt and black pepper to taste and keep warm.

2 Preheat the grill. Whip the remaining cream until stiff peaks form. Ladle the soup into heat-proof bowls and top each with a spoonful of whipped cream. Grill until just beginning to brown. Cool for a couple of minutes, then add a small quenelle (or ball) of caviar (do this with two teaspoons, transferring the caviar from one to the other until you have a good shape). Sprinkle with chopped parsley; serve immediately.

Serves 4

SERVE WITH *any good Chardonnay.*

SCALLOPS GRATINES WITH CAVIAR

You can use frozen scallops for this, but if you are able to buy fresh ones in season during the winter months you will obtain a better flavour.

1½ tbsp olive oil
175 g (6 oz) leeks (white part only),
washed, drained and finely chopped
salt and freshly ground black pepper
175 ml (6 fl oz) dry white wine
85 ml (3 fl oz) water
450 g (1 lb) Queen scallops (with the roe
removed), rinsed and dried
50 g (2 oz) unsalted butter, softened

50 g (2 oz) plain flour
85 ml (3 fl oz) plain yoghurt
2 slices white toasting bread
2 tbsp chives, freshly chopped
90 g (3 oz) Gruyère cheese, grated
90 g (3 oz) Sevruga caviar
dill sprigs to garnish, if desired

1 In a medium saucepan, heat the oil with the leeks, plus salt and pepper to taste. Stir over a moderate heat until the leek is soft but not coloured. Add the wine and water and bring to the boil. Reduce the liquid by half. Add the scallops and cook over a moderately high heat, stirring for 2–3 minutes or until they become opaque.

2 In a small bowl, mix the butter and flour to a smooth paste. Add it bit by bit to the scallop mixture, stirring constantly so that there are no lumps. Simmer for 2 minutes, stirring continually, then add the yoghurt, salt and pepper to taste and cook for another minute. (This mixture can be prepared the day before, cooled completely and stored in the refrigerator in a covered bowl; reheat when required.)

3 Preheat the grill. Using a cutter, cut out six rounds of bread about 3.5 cm (1½ in) in diameter. Toast on both sides, then place on a wire rack.

4 Stir the chives into the scallops, then divide the mixture between six ovenproof ramekins or gratin dishes. Sprinkle each dish with some of the grated Gruyère. Place the dishes on a baking dish about 10 cm (4 in) from the grill for 3–5 minutes, or until the Gruyère is melted and golden.

5 Place a heaped teaspoonful of caviar on each round of toast, then position this on top of the gratin dish. Garnish with dill and serve immediately.

Serves 4

SERVE WITH *top white burgundy, demi-sec Vouvray or Mosel Riesling Kabinett.*

SMOKED SALMON TARTARE WITH CAVIAR

A fresh-flavoured dish that requires very little culinary skill – an ideal choice on a hot summer's day for a starter or main course. The tartare can be made the day before you require it.

250 g (8 oz) smoked salmon
1 lime (or lemon)
1 medium red onion, finely chopped
30 capers, finely chopped
120 ml (4 fl oz) sour cream
salt and black pepper
12 chicory leaves, or ½ a cucumber, peeled and finely sliced
50 ml (2 fl oz) crème fraîche
50 g (2 oz) Sevruga caviar

1 Cut the smoked salmon into small dice. Using a paring knife, cut off strips of zest from the lime (or lemon). Slice it into thin julienne strips and blanch for a few seconds in boiling water, to retain its colour. Strain and set aside.

2 Squeeze the juice from the lime (or lemon) into a pudding bowl, then add the salmon, onion, capers, sour cream and seasoning. Mix well, then press down firmly and place in the refrigerator for at least ½ hour.

3 To serve, gently ease the tartare mixture from the pudding bowl, turning it upside-down onto a plate. Decorate with the zest of lime

(or lemon) strips, and surround with the chicory leaves or cucumber. Top with the crème fraîche and caviar. Serve with fresh toast or a tasty bread.

4 You can also make individual portions by dividing the mixture. Fill an 8 cm (3 in) round metal cutter with the filling. Gently ease it onto each plate and decorate as above.

Serves 4

SERVE WITH *NV Champagne, Sancerre/Pouilly-Fumé, Alsace, Clare Valley Riesling or vodka.*

SMOKED SALMON, FRENCH BEAN AND CAVIAR SALAD

If you can obtain smoked-salmon fillet, which is the central, sweetest and prime part of the salmon, it greatly enhances this dish.

150 g (5 oz) very fine French beans, topped and tailed
1 tbsp red wine vinegar
1 tsp lemon juice
120 ml (4 fl oz) virgin olive oil
salt and black pepper
2 shallots, finely chopped
300 g (11 oz) smoked-salmon fillet
100 g (4 oz) Sevruga caviar

1 Blanch the beans in a saucepan of boiling water for 1 minute, then drain and refresh in cold water. Dry on kitchen paper and cut in half.

2 To make the dressing, whisk the vinegar and lemon juice in a salad bowl. Gradually whisk in the oil, with salt and pepper to taste. Add the shallots and the beans. Cover and marinate for ½ hour.

3 Cut the salmon fillet crossways into slices about 1 cm (½ in) thick, allowing three slices per person. Remove the beans from the marinade with a slotted spoon and make a mound in the centre of each plate. Place three slices of salmon around the beans and fill in between with a teaspoonful of caviar.

Serves 4

SERVE WITH *NV Champagne, Fumé Blanc, Graves/Pessac-Léognan, Alsace Pinot Gris.*

DEEP-FRIED GOAT'S CHEESE WITH SALMON EGGS AND SALAD

This will melt in your mouth! On most cheese counters you can find goat's cheese logs. Choose a mild one that will easily slice into rounds.

1 small mild goat's cheese log
1 egg
freshly ground black pepper
40 g (1½ oz) breadcrumbs
600 ml (1 pt) light oil (sunflower or soya)
mixed leaf salad
30 g (1 oz) salmon eggs

1 Cut the cheese into 1 cm (½ in)-wide slices. Beat the egg with the pepper and pour it onto a small plate. Put the breadcrumbs on another plate. Dip the goat's cheese into the egg mixture and then roll it in the breadcrumbs, until thoroughly coated.

2 Heat the oil in a deep-fryer (taking care that it is not too hot or it will spit the breadcrumbs back out at you). Fry the cheese slices until golden brown. Remove and drain on kitchen paper.

3 To serve, arrange plates with salad leaves, then place three goat's cheese slices on each one. Top with a teaspoonful of salmon roe.

Serves 4

SERVE WITH *Sancerre/Pouilly-Fumé, Chablis or good Chenin Blanc (ie Savennières or dry Vouvray).*

BLINIS AND TORTILLAS

We have included two basic types of blinis for using in the "traditional" way of serving caviar (*see* page 102). Blinis are quite easy to make, although it is now also possible to buy good quality ready-made ones, both small and large, from most good food shops and supermarkets. Blinis freeze well and are best reheated in the microwave, for just a couple of seconds, as they tend to dry out quickly in the oven. You can make blinis any size you want – the recipes given below will serve 6–8 people, depending on the size of pancake that you make.

PLAIN BLINIS

These have a smooth texture unlike the rougher consistency of buckwheat blinis. For a variation, finely chop an onion and add it to the batter.

200 g (7 oz) plain flour, sifted
¼ tsp salt
3 eggs
400 ml (14 fl oz) semi-skimmed milk
50 g (2 oz) butter

1 Put the flour, salt, eggs and milk in a blender or food processor. Blend for 1–2 minutes until smooth. (You can also do this in a large mixing bowl, but it takes a bit longer and you have to beat very hard.) Strain the batter through a fine sieve into a jug and let it stand for ½ hour. These blinis contain no yeast, so they hardly rise.

2 Melt the butter in a small saucepan and pour a little into a large, non-stick frying pan. Pour enough of the batter into the pan to make four blinis about 2–3 mm (⅛ in) thick. Allow them to cook over a moderate heat for about 10 minutes on each side. When the blinis are lightly golden, transfer them to a wire rack, piling them loosely on top of each other to keep them moist. Keep them warm in a low oven while making four more blinis, remembering to add a little more melted butter to the pan as necessary. Alternatively, you can tip all the mixture into a large frying pan and cook slowly for about 20 minutes on each side. Remove and allow to cool a little on a wire rack, then cut into portions.

Serves 6–8

BUCKWHEAT AND
PLAIN FLOUR BLINIS

In Russia they used to make blinis just out of buckwheat flour, but it is quite strong
and slightly bitter, so mixing it with plain flour dilutes the flavour.

250–300 ml (8–10 fl oz) milk

1½ tsp dried yeast or 10 g
(¼ oz) fresh yeast

4 tbsp luke-warm water
(if using fresh yeast)

50 g (2 oz) plain flour

100 g (4 oz) buckwheat flour

½ tsp salt

50 g (2 oz) butter, plus
extra for frying

2 eggs, separated

2 tbsp sour cream

1 Pour 175 ml (6 fl oz) of the milk into a
saucepan. Heat until the milk rises, then
remove from the heat and allow to cool. If you
are using fresh yeast, mix it with the water,
then leave for 5 minutes until the surface is
covered in bubbles. Sift the flours and salt into
a bowl. Mix thoroughly. If you are using dried
yeast, add it now; otherwise make a well in the
flour and add the fresh yeast and water. Add the
luke-warm milk to the well. Gradually
incorporate the flour, beating the mixture for
2 minutes until smooth. Cover with a damp
cloth and put in a warm place for 2–3 hours,
until risen and full of bubbles.

2 Melt half the butter in a saucepan and allow
it to cool a little. Add a further 50 ml (2 fl oz)
milk to the risen batter, stirring it in thoroughly.
Blend in the egg yolks, sour cream and melted
butter and beat until the mixture has the
consistency of double cream. If it seems too
thick to pour, add a little more milk.

3 Whisk the egg whites until stiff peaks form.
Fold them into the batter, a little at a time,
cutting and folding them into the mixture until
they are thoroughly combined. Heat half the
remaining butter in a frying pan. Pour enough
batter into the pan to make equal-sized blinis –
small, medium or large. Turn them over when
they are lightly browned and cook on the other
side. Set aside to keep warm. Top up the pan
with a little butter as necessary.

Serves 6–8

TORTILLA CORNETS WITH SMOKED SALMON AND CAVIAR SALSA

This is a very simple dish. It looks delicious and is extremely easy to prepare. You can buy very good wheat tortillas in most supermarkets, so for the busy person this recipe is ideal.

100 g (3½ oz) smoked salmon
100 ml (3½ fl oz) crème fraîche
½ red onion, finely chopped
3 eggs, hard-boiled for 10 minutes and finely chopped
freshly ground black pepper
8–12 flour tortillas
8–12 cocktail sticks
50 g (2 oz) Sevruga caviar
50 g (2 oz) salmon roe
fresh green salad leaves
dill or chives, chopped
lemon wedges to garnish

1 Chop the smoked salmon into small pieces. In a mixing bowl, combine it with the crème fraîche, onion, eggs and pepper. Place in the refrigerator to stiffen for at least ½ hour.

2 Taking a tortilla, roll it into a cone and hold it up in your hand. Fill with the mixture and secure with a cocktail stick. Place one or two tortillas on each plate and fill the open ends with a teaspoonful of caviar and salmon eggs. Surround with salad leaves and garnish with dill or chives, and a lemon wedge.

Serves 4

SERVE WITH *Alsace or Clare Valley Riesling, vodka or lager.*

CAVIAR WITH TRADITIONAL ACCOMPANIMENTS

Some restaurants add small boiled potatoes to this dish, which work very well – *pommes de rats* in France or new Jersey Royals are the best for this.

2 large eggs
2 tbsp parsley, finely chopped
1 large red onion, very finely chopped
40–50 g (1½–2 oz) caviar per head (or more if you like)
150 ml (5 fl oz) sour cream
1 lemon, quartered

1 Put the eggs in a saucepan of cold, salted water and bring to the boil. Allow to simmer for 10 minutes, then plunge them into cold water for several minutes to cool. When the eggs are cold, shell them and carefully separate out the yolks. Keeping the whites and yolks apart, chop them finely.

2 On individual plates, arrange the hard-boiled egg whites, yolks, parsley and onion around the rim of the plate, leaving the centre for the caviar, which should be added just before serving. Place a spoonful of sour cream on each plate, or pass it round in a bowl. Garnish (if you must) with the lemon quarters. Serve with a plate of warmed blinis.

Serves 4

SERVE WITH *NV Champagne, good Sauvignon, unoaked Chardonnay or vodka.*

PASTRY DISHES

MILLEFEUILLE OF SMOKED SALMON, SALMON MOUSSE, FILO PASTRY AND CAVIAR

This makes a very exclusive "club sandwich".

8 sheets filo pastry
50 g (2 oz) butter, melted
8 large slices smoked salmon
100 g (3½ oz) smoked-salmon pieces
150 ml (5 fl oz) double cream
50 g (2 oz) chives, finely chopped
salt and black pepper
50 g (2 oz) Oscietre caviar

1 Preheat the oven to 220°C (425°F/Gas Mark 7). Carefully lay out the filo pastry and, using an 8 cm (3 in) metal cutter, cut out 24 rounds. Place 12 rounds evenly spaced on a baking dish. Brush with melted butter, then put another round of filo pastry directly on top. Bake for about 5 minutes, until golden brown. (It is very easy to burn these, so watch them carefully.) Leave to cool on a wire rack.

2 Spread out the slices of smoked salmon and, using the same cutter, cut out 12 rounds (three per person). Cover with clingfilm and set aside. Put all the smoked salmon pieces into a food processor and mince roughly. With the processor on a slow setting, gradually add the cream. Transfer the mixture to a bowl, mix in the chives, plus salt and pepper to taste, and put in the refrigerator until needed. To make the sauce, mix the sour cream with the chopped shallots and a little pepper.

3 To serve, place one double filo sheet on a plate, followed by a layer of the minced salmon mixture and a smoked salmon round. Repeat twice, for each person, so that each has a stack of three layers. Then generously top this exclusive "club sandwich" with caviar.

Serves 4

SERVE WITH *NV Champagne, Sancerre/ Pouilly-Fumé or Chablis.*

CREAMY SCRAMBLED EGGS WITH CAVIAR IN PASTRY CASES

You can also make this creamy dish in a 20 cm (8 in) round pastry case, instead of the individual tartlet pans suggested below.

30 g (1 oz) plain flour
1 packet (225 g/8 oz) shortcrust pastry
5 eggs
40 g (1½ oz) butter, plus extra to grease the tartlet pan
1 tsp crème fraîche
30 g (1 oz) smoked salmon, chopped
1 tbsp parsley, finely chopped
salt and black pepper
50 g (2 oz) Sevruga caviar

1 Preheat the oven to 180°C (350°F/Gas Mark 4). Butter some tartlet pans. On a floured board, roll out the pastry and cut it into rounds to fit your tartlet pans. Bake for approximately 15 minutes. Remove the pastry cases from the oven and place on a flat baking dish.

2 In a mixing bowl, lightly beat the eggs. Heat the butter in a saucepan, add the eggs, then stir gently over the heat until just beginning to set. Remove from the heat and immediately stir in the crème fraîche, followed by the smoked salmon, parsley and some freshly ground pepper and a little salt.

3 Spoon the mixture into the pastry cases, keeping them warm in a low oven. Just before serving, top them with the caviar.

Serves 4

***SERVE WITH** rosé Champagne or Chablis Premier Cru.*

SMOKED COD AND CAVIAR VOL-AU-VENTS

You can use any small-sized pastry case and simply add this delicious filling.

100 g (3½ oz) smoked cod, skinned and boned
120 ml (4 fl oz) milk
2 egg yolks
1 tbsp mayonnaise
1 tbsp chives, finely chopped
1 tbsp parsley, finely chopped
100 g (3½ oz) Emmenthal or Gruyère cheese, grated
½ tsp Dijon mustard
1 packet of puff-pastry mini vol-au-vents (allowed to defrost) or 8 large pastry cases
1 egg white
125 g (4½ oz) Sevruga caviar

1 Preheat the oven to the temperature given on the puff-pastry packet. Poach the smoked cod in the milk for 5 minutes. Drain and cool. Blend the fish, egg yolks and mayonnaise. Transfer to a mixing bowl and stir in the herbs, cheese and mustard. Mix well. This can be stored covered in the refrigerator for three hours.

2 Cook the vol-au-vent as instructed on the packet (less 5 minutes so that they are not too golden). Cut out the lids and discard.

3 Beat the egg white until soft peaks form, then fold into the fish mixture. Spoon into the cases and bake at 180°C (350° F/Gas Mark 4) for 10 minutes. Remove from the oven and allow to cool. Place a teaspoonful of caviar on top of each case and serve.

Serves 4

***SERVE WITH** Pouilly-Fuissé, Sauvignon-Sémillon blends or Fumé Blanc.*

CAVIAR AND PRAWN BASKETS

This recipe offers an interesting surprise as the caviar is hidden beneath the prawn mixture.
You can also use salmon or trout eggs.

2 large sheets of filo pastry
40 g (1½ oz) butter, melted
120 ml (4 fl oz) single cream
120 ml (4 fl oz) milk
1 tbsp cornflour
10 large cooked prawns
1 tsp Dijon mustard
1 tbsp parsley, finely chopped
salt and black pepper
125 g (4½ oz) Oscietre caviar

1 Preheat the oven to 200°C (400°F/Gas Mark 6). Cut each sheet of pastry into strips about 7 cm (2¾ in) wide. Cut each strip into squares, then cover with a clean damp cloth. Brush four squares with melted butter, layer them together at an angle, then gently push them into small, greased tartlet pans to make basket shapes. Repeat with the remaining squares and butter. Bake for about 5 minutes or until lightly browned. Remove the pastry baskets from the pans and place on a wire rack to cool. The baskets can be baked up to two days before they are needed.

2 In a saucepan, thoroughly mix together the cream and milk with the cornflour, then add the chopped prawns and bring to the boil, stirring constantly until the mixture thickens. Add the mustard, parsley and seasoning. Cool to room temperature.

3 Just before serving, place a teaspoonful of caviar into a filo basket with a teaspoonful of the prawn mixture on top. Bake in a preheated oven at 180°C (350°F/Gas Mark 4) for 5 minutes.

Serves 4

SERVE WITH *vintage Champagne or top white burgundy (ie Puligny-Montrachet).*

SALMON TART TOPPED WITH CAVIAR

For this moreish tart you can either make your own pastry, or alternatively buy one of the excellent frozen pastries that are now readily available. To serve 4–6 people, use a 23 cm (9 in) non-stick flan dish.

Pastry
175 g (6 oz) plain flour
100 g (3½ oz) butter, at room temperature
1 egg yolk
3–4 tbsp chilled water
pinch of salt

Filling
200 g (7 oz) salmon, boned and skinned
500 g (1½ lb) fresh spinach, or 200 g (7 oz) frozen whole-leaf spinach
25 g (1 oz) butter, softened
1 egg
1 egg yolk
100 ml (3½ fl oz) milk
125 g (4½ oz) cream cheese
salt and black pepper
pinch of nutmeg
100 g (3½ oz) Sevruga caviar

1 Preheat the oven to 220°C (425°F/Gas Mark 7). Put the flour in a mixing bowl. Dice the butter and add it to the flour, kneading it with your fingers. Add the egg yolk, water and salt. Mix well and cover with foil. Place in the refrigerator for about 1 hour.

2 Butter a flan tin. Lightly flour a large board and roll out the chilled pastry to make a 30 cm (12 in) circle. Roll the dough around the rolling pin, then drape it over the tin, so that it overlaps the edges. Gently press the pastry down into the flan tin. Using a sharp knife, trim the edges. Prick the base lightly with a fork, to prevent air bubbles forming. Place in the refrigerator for around 15 minutes. Cut a sheet of foil a little larger than the flan dish and place it on top of the pastry shell. Weigh it down with rice or dried beans. Bake for around 15 minutes or until the pastry begins to brown. Remove the foil and beans, then reduce the oven to 190°C (375°F/Gas Mark 5) and cook for another 5–8 minutes. Remove the tart from the oven, but leave the oven on.

3 To make the filling, cut the salmon into strips. Remove the stems from the fresh spinach and rinse in cold water (frozen spinach should be defrosted and drained). In a large saucepan, heat the butter and cook the fresh spinach for 3–4 minutes until it breaks down. Remove from heat and allow to cool. (The frozen spinach does not need to be cooked before being used.)

4 In a bowl, place the egg, egg yolk, milk and cream cheese; season to taste and add the nutmeg. Beat together, then mix in the salmon strips.

5 Spread the spinach over the pastry shell, then pour over the quiche mixture almost to the rim of the flan tin. Bake the tart for about ½ hour, until lightly browned. If you pierce it with a skewer that comes out of the tart cleanly, it is cooked. Allow to cool, then spread with caviar and serve in slices. Accompany with a salad of chicory and watercress.

Serves 4

SERVE WITH *NV Champagne, Pouilly-Fuissé or white Bordeaux (ie Graves/Pessac-Léognan).*

EGG DISHES

FLUFFY CAVIAR OMELETTE

This dish is fun to make, but is best done among good friends who are in or near your kitchen, as it must be served immediately it is finished. If you preheat your grill and two rings of your cooker prior to preparing the egg mixture, it is very quick to cook. You need two 20 cm (8 in) frying pans.

2 tbsp each of chives and parsley, chopped
200 ml (7 fl oz) fromage frais
½ tsp lemon juice
salt and freshly ground black pepper
125 g (4½ oz) smoked salmon, roughly chopped
125 g (4½ oz) Oscietre, Beluga or Sevruga caviar
8 large free-range eggs, separated
2 tbsp cold water
4 tbsp butter
parsley sprigs to garnish

1 Mix the chives and parsley into the fromage frais, with a few drops of lemon juice and some ground pepper. Get your smoked salmon and caviar ready, then set to one side until your omelettes are cooked. Preheat the grill and two cooker rings to a high temperature, and warm some plates.

2 In a medium-sized bowl, whisk the egg yolks with the cold water and seasoning. In a separate bowl, whisk the egg whites until stiff peaks form. Using a spatula, gently fold the whites into the yolk mixture.

3 Spoon 1 tbsp of butter into each frying pan and, when melted, pour quarter of the egg mixture into each pan, covering the base.

Cook for 1–2 minutes until the omelette turns a light golden brown. Then transfer the pans under the grill, just long enough for the omelette to puff up and set on top, browning slightly. Place immediately onto a heated dish and repeat the process as quickly as possible.

4 Taking each omelette, put quarter of the fromage frais mixture onto it, then put quarter of the smoked salmon on top. Carefully fold the omelette in half and top with a generous teaspoonful of caviar. Garnish with the parsley sprigs and serve with crisp toast of your choice.

Serves 4

SERVE WITH *NV Champagne, white burgundy or top Alsace Pinot Blanc.*

SCRAMBLED EGGS WITH
LOBSTER AND CAVIAR

Really good scrambled eggs are a delight – and perfect with caviar. They should have a
slightly creamy consistency and, if made correctly, are equally delicious hot or cold.
The lobster in this recipe gives them an added dimension of flavour and texture.

200 g (7 oz) unsalted butter
150 ml (5 fl oz) water
1 lobster
8 eggs
100 ml (3½ fl oz) double cream
salt and freshly ground black pepper
baby salad leaves to garnish
50 g (2 oz) Beluga caviar

1 Melt the butter in a saucepan. Add 50 ml
(1½ fl oz) water to prevent the lobster burning,
then put in the lobster claws. Simmer for 5
minutes, covered. Add the tail and continue to
simmer for another 4 minutes. Remove the
lobster with a slotted spoon, then set aside until
cool enough to take out the lobster meat from
the tail and claws, reserving the shells. Cook
the shells in the existing butter with another
100 ml (3½ fl oz) water, uncovered, until the
water has evaporated. Strain the liquid butter
through a fine sieve, discarding the shells, and
allow to cool.

2 In a mixing bowl, beat the eggs together
with the cream, seasoning and the cooled
lobster butter. Shred the lobster meat into small
pieces, reserving two whole claws.

3 Pour the eggs into a non-stick saucepan,
stirring continuously with a wooden spoon.
When they are hot but not yet beginning to set,
add the lobster meat and stir until you have a
thick, creamy consistency.

4 Serve on warm plates with some baby
salad leaves. Place the scrambled lobster
in the middle of the plate. Slice the reserved
claws in half and use to decorate each plate.
Crown the scrambled egg with caviar and serve
immediately.

Serves 4

SERVE WITH *top vintage Champagne.*

SCRAMBLED EGG WITH FRESH TRUFFLE AND CAVIAR ON BRIOCHE TOAST

The flavour and smell of fresh truffle and caviar combined with scrambled eggs makes a very exciting taste experience, which has to be tried to be believed!

8 free-range eggs
salt and freshly ground black pepper
30 g (1 oz) butter
1½ tbsp double cream
fresh brioche loaf for toasting
1 fresh truffle
50 g (2 oz) Beluga or Oscietre caviar

1 To make the scrambled egg, break the eggs into a bowl and season. Whisk vigorously until frothy. Heat the butter in a non-stick saucepan and pour in the eggs. Stir over a low heat with a wooden spoon until the eggs just begin to set, then take them off the heat and quickly add the cream, stirring continuously. Keep warm in the oven while you toast the brioche.

2 To serve, take four heated plates and make a mound of scrambled egg in the middle of each one. Using a sharp knife, cut very fine slices of truffle and arrange them on top. Then add a teaspoonful of caviar for each person. Serve with slices of freshly toasted brioche on the side.

Serves 4

SERVE WITH *with mature vintage Champagne.*

LIGHTLY BOILED EGGS WITH CAVIAR

The variations below are ideal for a romantic breakfast, a light starter or simply for a treat.

1 Boil a large, free-range egg for 6 minutes. Cut off the top with a serrated knife, then crown the egg with 10 g (¼ oz) Beluga caviar per person. Serve with fingers of white toast. The caviar eggs blend and mix with the hen's egg deliciously.

Another, rich variation is as follows:
4 large free-range eggs
1 tsp shallots, finely chopped
salt and white pepper
65 ml (2½ fl oz) crème fraîche
1 tsp chives, finely chopped, plus whole chives to garnish
60 g (2 oz) Oscietre caviar

1 Carefully slice the tops off the eggs with a serrated knife and tip the contents into a bowl. Wash and gently dry the shells and set them aside. Lightly beat the eggs, then pour them into a non-stick saucepan over a gentle heat with the shallots. Using a whisk, beat them vigorously until they just start to thicken. Remove from the heat, season to taste, then add the crème fraîche and chopped chives.

2 Place the shells in eggcups, then fill each shell three-quarters full with the egg mixture. Cut the whole chives into 5 cm (2 in) lengths and make a fan shape with 4–5 of them, placing them upright into the filling to one side of the egg. Put a heaped teaspoonful of caviar (15 g/ ½ oz per egg) on top and serve immediately.

Serves 4

SERVE WITH *vintage Champagne.*

POACHED HEN'S EGG WITH CAVIAR ON PUREED POTATO WITH HOLLANDAISE

The Hollandaise makes a perfect foil to the puréed potato in this
sumptuous dish.

450 g (1 lb) potatoes
50 g (2 oz) salted butter
salt and freshly ground black pepper
2 tbsp single cream
120 ml (4 fl oz) milk
2 spring onions, finely snipped (optional)
Hollandaise sauce (see page 148)
4 large free-range eggs
2 tbsp of white vinegar (if not using an egg poacher)
125 g (4½ oz) Sevruga caviar

1 Peel and slice the potatoes. Bring to the boil in a large saucepan of salted water and simmer for around 20 minutes, or until tender. Drain the water off and, using a potato masher, mash them hard until the potato is well crushed. Add the butter, a generous pinch of salt and lots of black pepper. Continue mashing until the mixture is smooth and there are no lumps. Then add the cream and milk, plus the spring onions (if desired), and work in well with a fork. Beat the mixture again hard until it is fluffy and creamy. Set aside and keep hot.

2 Make the Hollandaise sauce. Half-fill a non-stick egg poacher with water and bring to simmering point. Grease the individual pans with a little butter. Break the eggs into the poacher and season with pepper. Simmer, covered, for 3 minutes or until the eggs are no longer translucent. Alternatively, fill a deep saucepan three-quarters full of water with 2 tbsp of white vinegar. Bring to a brisk boil, then lower to just simmering. Break and drop in the eggs as required. As each egg goes into the water, immediately push the white back towards the yolk, moving the egg gently. Simmer each egg for 3 minutes. Remove with a slotted spoon and place on kitchen paper to drain.

3 On four heated plates, arrange a mound of puréed potato. Pour the Hollandaise sauce around the potato and place an egg on top of each mound. Divide the caviar into four equal portions and spoon on top of the eggs.

Serves 4

SERVE WITH *NV Champagne, Premier or Grand Cru Chablis.*

QUAIL EGGS IN DEEP-FRIED VEGETABLE NESTS WITH CAVIAR

This makes an impressive-looking, light starter.

16 quail eggs
2 medium carrots
2 medium celeriac
juice of 1 lemon
300 ml (10 fl oz) light oil (sunflower)
200 ml (7 fl oz) single cream
200 ml (7 fl oz) sour cream
salt and black pepper
4 tbsp chives, finely chopped,
plus whole chives to garnish
baby leaf salad to garnish
50 g (2 oz) Beluga caviar

1 Bring a saucepan of water to the boil. Place the quail eggs into the water in a wire basket for 1½ minutes. Then plunge them into cold water and peel.

2 If you have an automatic grater on your food processor, grate the carrots and the celeriac into long, thin julienne strips. If not, try to grate or slice the vegetables as thinly as possible. Put them into a bowl with half the lemon juice.

3 In a deep-fat fryer with a wire basket, heat the oil. Drain the vegetables well and pat dry on kitchen paper. Twist the vegetable julienne strips into bird's nest shapes and place in the wire basket. When the oil is hot, plunge in the "nests" and deep-fry for 1 minute. Lift out of the oil, and drain well on layers of kitchen paper.

4 Mix the single cream with the sour cream and the remaining lemon juice, then season to taste. Whisk vigorously until the mixture stiffens a little, then stir in the chopped chives.

5 To serve, decorate four plates with a baby leaf salad, lightly tossed in oil with a few drops of balsamic vinegar. In the centre of each plate, place one nest filled with 4 quail eggs. Generously coat the eggs with the cream sauce and top each nest with quarter of the caviar. Cut the whole chives into 6 cm (2½ in) lengths and make a fan shape with 4–5 of them, placing them upright between the eggs.

Serves 4

SERVE WITH *NV Champagne, white Bordeaux (ie Graves/Pessac-Léognan) or Sauvignon Blanc (ie Sancerre/Pouilly-Fumé).*

POTATO DISHES

POTATO SALAD WITH CAVIAR

This is a delicious accompaniment to any seafood, especially cold lobster.

450 g (1 lb) waxy potatoes
75 g (3 oz) chopped chives
200 ml (7 fl oz) mayonnaise
freshly ground black pepper
30 g (1 oz) Sevruga caviar

1 Wash and peel the potatoes, leaving them whole. Bring a large pan of salted water to the boil. Cook the potatoes for about 20 minutes. Drain and set aside to cool.

2 When the potatoes are cool, cut them into 3 mm (⅛ in) slices. Using a cutter, cut out 2½ cm (1 in) rounds. In a bowl, combine the potatoes, chives, mayonnaise and pepper (you may wish to add a little salt, but the caviar is already slightly salty, so take care not to overdo it). Lastly, very gently fold in the caviar, leaving 1 tsp with which to garnish the top. The potato salad can be made several hours in advance and refrigerated, but do not fold in the caviar until you intend to serve it.

Serves 4

SERVE WITH *NV Champagne, Alsace Pinot Blanc, good white burgundy or white Bordeaux.*

BAKED POTATO TOPPED WITH CAVIAR

This is a very simple dish, but it can be something very special. A charismatic English lord woos his girlfriends with the most superb baked potatoes, piled high with Beluga caviar. His success rate is high – and the buzz even better!

2 large old potatoes
75 g (3 oz) salted butter
2 tbsp (or more) crème fraîche or sour cream
½ red onion, very finely chopped (optional)
125–250 g (4½–9 oz) Beluga caviar

1 Preheat the oven to 180°C (350°F/Gas Mark 4). Scrub the potatoes well, then prick them with a fork. Bake for 1½–2 hours until crisp on the outside and soft and flaky on the inside. Cut the potatoes open, squeeze the sides together, top with the butter and let it melt into the potato. Put 1 tbsp of crème fraîche or sour cream on top, plus 1 tbsp of red onion if desired, then pile on the caviar.

Serves 2

SERVE WITH *a bottle of fine rosé Champagne – this should really get passions running high!*

POTATO PANCAKES WITH CAVIAR AND BEURRE BLANC WHITE WINE SAUCE

Potato pancakes come in many forms. This recipe makes a rich and rather sinful starter and needs to be followed by a fairly plain main course. The combination of pancake, caviar and the white wine sauce is quite sublime.

500 g (1¼ lb) potatoes
50 ml (2 fl oz) milk
beurre blanc white wine sauce (see page 142)
75 g (3 oz) plain flour, plus extra to flour the board
½ tsp salt
½ tsp baking powder
150 g (5 oz) butter
50 ml (2 fl oz) double cream
50 g (2 oz) Sevruga or Oscietre caviar
chives, cut into 2.5 cm (1 in) lengths

1 Peel the potatoes, then slice and cook them in boiling salted water for around 20–25 minutes. Drain well and purée with the milk. Allow to cool.

2 Make the beurre blanc white wine sauce and keep hot.

3 In a large bowl, sift together the flour, salt and baking powder. Rub in 50 g (2 oz) of the butter, then work in the puréed potatoes, followed by the cream. Knead the mixture a little with your fingers, then divide into six balls. Roll each ball out on a floured board to a thickness of about 5 mm (¼ in) and cut in half. Heat 50 g (2 oz) butter in a large saucepan and, over a low heat, cook the pancakes for 8–10 minutes on both sides until nicely browned. Make sure they are cooked right through, but take care that they do not burn, as they cook

very quickly. You may have to do this in two batches, adding more butter for frying in between. Place the pancakes on a heated dish and keep hot in the oven.

4 Taking some warmed plates, place a pancake on each one, then divide the beurre blanc white wine sauce over each pancake, so that it overflows on and around it. Place a second potato cake on top and put a generous tsp of caviar on top of that. Garnish with a sprinkling of chopped chives. Serve immediately.

Serves 4

SERVE WITH *vintage Champagne, top white burgundy or Alsace Pinot Blanc.*

POTATO ROSTIS WITH SMOKED SALMON, QUAIL EGGS AND CAVIAR

These potato pancakes make a perfect lunch or light supper dish.

Röstis
450 g (1 lb) potatoes
1 red onion, grated
2 egg yolks
salt and black pepper
olive oil for frying

Topping
4 quail eggs
65 ml (2½ fl oz) crème fraîche
100 g (3½ oz) smoked salmon, diced
100 g (3½ oz) Sevruga or Oscietre caviar

1 Peel the potatoes and grate them raw into a bowl. Rinse well, drain, then wrap them in a clean towel to draw out the remaining moisture. Return them to the bowl and mix in the onion, egg yolks and seasoning. Heat a little olive oil in a frying pan. Divide the potato mixture into eight balls, then flatten them out slightly. Fry over a moderate heat for around 10 minutes on either side, until golden brown. Remove from the pan, drain on kitchen paper and transfer to a plate in a warm oven.

2 Heat the frying pan with a little more oil, then carefully break the quail eggs into it and fry until cooked (about 1–2 minutes). Set them aside to keep warm.

3 Warm 4 plates and put 2 röstis on each. Place a spoonful of crème fraîche on one rösti and pile on a quarter of the smoked salmon. Pop a quail egg onto the other rösti and top with 2 tsp of caviar. Serve immediately.

Serves 4

SERVE WITH *Champagne, top Sauvignon Blanc, fino sherry or vodka.*

DEEP-FRIED POTATO BALLS
FILLED WITH CAVIAR

The way these potato balls are made results in a quick final frying time, which means
the caviar does not have time to cook, so is unaffected by the process. Sevruga is
the best caviar for this, because if it is heated slightly the eggs will not be damaged –
unlike the more delicate caviar varieties.

450 g (1 lb) potatoes

2 eggs

salt and black pepper

250 ml (8 fl oz) sour cream

1 tsp lemon juice

100 g (3½ oz) Sevruga caviar

450 ml (15 fl oz) light cooking oil (sunflower or soya)

4 tbsp fresh, dried breadcrumbs

225 g (8 oz) marinated smoked sturgeon (see page 145);
if this is unavailable, use smoked salmon
or smoked trout

salad leaves to garnish

1 Bring a large saucepan of salted water to
the boil. Peel, rinse and slice the potatoes, then
simmer for about 20 minutes until cooked.
Drain and mash with one beaten egg. Season
and set aside to cool.

2 Mix most of the sour cream with the
lemon juice and season with a little pepper.
Refrigerate until required.

3 When the mashed potato is at room
temperature, take a tablespoonful and, with
your hands, roll it into balls about the size of a
golf ball. Using a sharp knife, cut each ball in
half and hollow out a well in the centre. Fill
with a teaspoonful of caviar. Put the halves
together again and gently remould until they
stick together. You should have enough for two
potato balls each.

4 Heat a deep-fat fryer containing light
cooking oil until it is nearly bubbling.

5 On one plate beat the remaining egg; on
another plate spread out the breadcrumbs.
Roll the potato balls in the beaten egg and then
in the breadcrumbs. Deep-fry them for about
1 minute, or until golden brown. Remove with
a slotted spoon and drain on kitchen paper.
Keep warm.

6 To serve, arrange the marinated smoked
sturgeon on plates, adding one complete potato
ball and cutting the other in half to reveal the
caviar. Garnish with salad leaves.

Serves 4

SERVE WITH *NV Champagne, good white
burgundy, other fine Chardonnay or vodka.*

PASTA

SPAGHETTINI WITH CAVIAR AND CHAMPAGNE SAUCE

This dish combines the simplicity of pasta with the exotic nature of both Champagne and caviar, to stunning effect.

300 ml (10 fl oz) clear stock
1 glass Champagne
1 sprig thyme
1 shallot, finely chopped
pinch of grated nutmeg
300 ml (10 fl oz) double cream
30 g (1 oz) cold butter, diced
salt and freshly ground black pepper
1 tbsp white wine vinegar
125 g (4½ oz) Sevruga caviar
1 tbsp olive oil
1 packet (500 g/1¼ lb) spaghettini

1 Bring the stock to boil, then add the Champagne, thyme, shallot and nutmeg. Reduce by three-quarters. Add the cream and simmer for 5 minutes. Take off the heat and strain into a bowl sitting in a *bain marie* or pan or hot water. Vigorously whisk in the butter, seasoning and vinegar. Keep warm until just before serving, then add the caviar.

2 Bring a large saucepan of water to the boil with ½ tsp salt and 1 tbsp oil. Cook the spaghettini following the instructions on the packet. Drain and tip into a large, heated bowl. Pour over the Champagne caviar sauce and serve immediately.

Serves 4

SERVE WITH with Champagne, white burgundy or Pinot Blanc or Pinot Bianco.

HOME-MADE CRAB AND SCALLOP TORTELLINI WITH CAVIAR

These tortellini are surprisingly easy to make yourself, using pasta sheets bought ready-made, and look sensational combined with the crab and scallops.

4 large scallops
100 g (3½ oz) crabmeat, shredded
2 shallots, finely chopped
zest of ½ lemon
1 tsp fresh root ginger, finely chopped
salt and freshly ground black pepper
150 g (5 oz) fresh pasta sheets
1 tbsp oil
1 cucumber, peeled and cut into thin julienne strips
50 g (2 oz) Oscietre caviar

Sauce
200 ml (7 fl oz) fish stock
50 g (2 oz) lobster or langoustine shells (if possible)
2 sticks lemongrass
zest of 1 lemon
100 ml (3½ fl oz) single cream
100 g (3½ oz) cold butter, diced
salt and black pepper

1 To make the tortellini, roughly chop the scallops, without the orange roe (save this for the sauce). In a bowl combine the scallops with the crabmeat, shallots, lemon zest and ginger. Season to taste.

2 Spread out the pasta sheets and using a cutter, stamp out 16 discs of approximately 8 cm (3 in) in size. Place a small tsp of the crab and scallop mixture onto each disc. Using a pastry brush, brush water on two edges of the square, then fold these over to make a semi-circle. To form the tortellini, wrap the pasta around your finger, wet both the corners and pinch them together. Put the tortellini aside, while you make the sauce.

3 In a saucepan combine the fish stock, shells, the orange roe of the scallops and the lemongrass and bring to a rapid boil. Reduce the liquid by half. Strain, add the lemon zest and reduce down again to 2 tbsp of "syrup".

Pour in the cream, then bring back to the boil and rapidly whisk in the diced butter, bit by bit, until frothy. Season. Strain through a fine sieve and keep warm.

4 Bring a large pan of salted water, with 1 tbsp of oil, to the boil and drop in the tortellini. Cook for around 8 minutes or until *al dente*.

5 To serve, take four warm plates and make a small heap of the julienne of cucumber in the centre of each one. Place four tortellini around each mound. Pour the sauce over the tortellini and top the centre with a generous teaspoonful of caviar. Serve immediately.

Serves 4

SERVE WITH *vintage Champagne, Mosel Riesling Kabinett or white Bordeaux (ie Graves/Pessac-Léognan).*

SUSHI AND FISH

Sushi has become devastatingly chic and popular all over the world. All the ingredients for sushi must be absolutely fresh; the same goes for sashimi, which is a generic term for thinly sliced raw fish.

FISH EGGS FOR SUSHI

When selecting ingredients for sushi, try to buy a range of different fish eggs. You can order these from a fishmonger or Japanese food shop. Several kinds of roe are imported from Japan, and most of these are processed. Below are some of the roe most often used for sushi:

Ikura salmon roe

Uni sea-urchin roe (when in season)

Kazunoko herring roe

Tobiko flying-fish roe

Ebikko smelt roe

cod's roe

plus, of course, the caviar of your choice.

Top each piece of sushi with a generous helping of fish eggs and, for colour and variety, add other smoked or raw fish. Even an amateur can make these sushi look attractive and interesting, although the speed and skill of a professional Japanese chef have to be seen to be believed.

OTHER SPECIALIST SUSHI INGREDIENTS & UTENSILS

You will need to visit a Japanese food shop for some of the other sushi ingredients and, if you are really enthusiastic, for selected cooking utensils, too. A few of the specialist ingredients that you will need are:

Good-quality short-grained or Japanese rice

Bottle of rice vinegar

Bottle of Saki, a sweetish Japanese rice wine

Nori (dried laver), a seaweed that comes in a vacuum pack

Gari, sweet pickled ginger

Wasabi, green horseradish

Kombu, dried kelp, for flavouring the rice

Soy sauce, for dipping your sushi in

You may also wish to buy a *makisu*, which is used for rolling out the rice and other ingredients. It is a mat made of bamboo strips attached together by string. You can buy various sizes, depending on what you are making, but start with one of about 20 cm (8 in). A wooden bowl called a *handai* is used to cool the rice, but you can equally use a ceramic bowl. You also need a wooden spoon or spatula.

STICKY RICE

First, you need to make the sticky rice, which is the base for all sushi and its derivatives. This recipe is really best measured in "cups", one cup usually corresponding to 200 ml (7 fl oz) of liquid or 215 g (7½ oz) of rice.

3 cups short-grained rice
3 tbsp sweet Saki
3 cups water
8 cm (3 in) square Kombu

Vinegar mixture
6 tbsp rice vinegar
2 tbsp white sugar
2 tsp sweet Saki
2 tsp salt

1 Place the rice in a fine sieve and wash it well until the water runs clear. Leave to drain for about 30 minutes.

2 Put the rice, Saki and water into an electric rice cooker or non-stick saucepan, together with the square of Kombu (scored with a knife to release its flavour). Bring to the boil, then simmer for 10 minutes. Remove the Kombu and discard. Turn out the rice into a ceramic or glass bowl (or a pre soaked *handai*).

3 In another saucepan, heat the ingredients for the vinegar mixture and stir until the sugar has dissolved. Take care not to boil.

4 While the rice is still hot, pour over the vinegar mixture and, using a spatula or wooden spoon, mix them together quickly using vertical cutting movements. At this point, in Japan, you would fan the rice while mixing it, to cool it down. Then cover the bowl with a damp cloth until you use it to make the sushi.

NORI-WRAPPED SUSHI ROLLS

In Japan these are made on a bamboo map called a *makisu*. A wooden board can suffice equally well for the purpose.

1 packet Nori
pre-cooked sticky rice (see left)
50 g (2 oz) Sevruga caviar
50 g (2 oz) salmon roe
50 g (2 oz) whatever alternative fish roe you can obtain, from those listed on page 126

1 On a board, cut a sheet of Nori in half lengthways and lay the shiny side down. Spread a layer of cooked rice over the Nori, leaving a 1 cm (½ in) space around all the edges. Carefully roll the Nori and rice into a tight cylinder, pushing one edge of the Nori onto the other and sticking it down onto it.

2 Allow to stand for 20 minutes. Repeat, making as many cylinders as you require. Then, using a sharp knife, cut the rolls into 2.5 cm (1 in) bite-sized pieces. Using a teaspoon, and holding the seam of each rolled piece so that it does not come unrolled, make an indentation in the top of the rice and fill it with half caviar and half the other fish roe of your choice. Repeat until you have an attractively filled and colourful selection of rolls.

HAND-PRESSED RICE SAUSAGES

The roes for this dish should be those that come in a dense mass, such as cod, herring or sea-urchin roe. You can add some fresh prawns (split wide open), very fresh raw or marinated fish and even smoked sturgeon, salmon or eel.

pre-cooked sticky rice (see page 127)
Wasabi, peeled and chopped, then crushed into a paste
50 g (2 oz) each of 3–4 different roes or fish
1 packet Nori
Gari, to garnish

1 In your hand, roll short sausages out of the rice about the size of two joints of a finger. On top of your rice sausage, spread a thin layer of Wasabi, then place roe or a piece of fish on top, large enough to cover the surface.

2 Using a sharp knife, cut strips of Nori about 1 cm (½ in) wide and long enough to wind around the rice and its topping. Garnish with Gari.

PRESSED, SHAPED RICE SUSHI

For this variation you need a small cutter, and you can alternate different shapes if you wish.

pre-cooked sticky rice (see page 127)
50 g (2 oz) each of 3–4 different roes

Press the rice down into the cutters, leaving a 5 mm (¼ in) gap at the top, which you then fill with fish roe. Carefully remove the cutter, and repeat as required using the different roes.

SERVE ALL SUSHI WITH saki, yamagata, Champagne or good Sauvignon Blanc, especially from New Zealand.

Clockwise from top left: Beluga, salmon roe, Tobiko (flying fish roe), Sevruga, salmon eggs.

CRAYFISH MOUSSE WITH CAVIAR
AND A CHIVE DRESSING

Crayfish, a freshwater crustacean, has become increasingly rare and expensive due to the fact that it cannot reproduce as quickly as it is caught; it does not reach adulthood until it is at least five years old. But its subtle flavour and delicate flesh distinguish it from lobsters and langoustines (Dublin Bay prawns), although these could be used as a substitute if no crayfish is available. Before cooking, it is always a good idea to remove the gut (the small black sack at the end of the tail) as this can taint the flavour. This luxurious mousse is perfect for a starter or even a light summer main course if served with salad.

1 kg (2¼ lb) crayfish (about 25)
50–250 g (2–9 oz) caviar

Stock
1 small onion
1 medium carrot
30 g (1 oz) butter
pinch of thyme
1 bay leaf
2 tbsp Cognac
2 tbsp dry white wine
350 ml (12 fl oz) light fish stock
salt and white pepper

Mousse
1 tbsp powdered gelatine
4 tbsp water; to dissolve gelatine
150 ml (5 fl oz) whipping cream
meat taken from the crayfish
1 tbsp lemon juice
½ tsp cayenne pepper
2 egg whites

Chive dressing
200 ml (7 fl oz) single cream
2 tbsp dry white wine
pinch of white pepper
1 bunch chives, finely snipped

1 Rinse the crayfish in cold water. Bring a large saucepan of salted water to the boil, then add the crayfish and cook for 5 minutes. Drain, set aside and allow to cool. Carefully peel the crayfish tails and the largest claws. Keep the shells for the stock. Set aside 10–12 tails for decoration.

2 To make the stock, roughly crush the reserved shells with a food mallet (best done in a double-thickness plastic bag). Peel and chop the onion and carrot. Heat the butter in a large saucepan and lightly fry the crushed shells, adding the onion, carrot, thyme and bay leaf. Heat the Cognac in a soup ladle and carefully set it alight. Pour it over the mixture. Put out the last flames with the white wine. Add the fish stock, season with salt and white pepper and allow to simmer, covered, for 20 minutes. Strain the liquid into another saucepan, using a very fine-meshed sieve. There should be about 350 ml (12 fl oz) of stock remaining. Allow to cool.

3 To make the mousse, place the gelatine and water in a bowl, over a saucepan of hot water, stirring until the gelatine has dissolved. Allow to cool. Whip the cream until it begins to thicken. Put it into a food processor with 150 ml (5 fl oz) of the fish stock you have just made. Pour the gelatine in a thin stream into the mixture. Add the crayfish meat, lemon juice and cayenne to season, then blend together. Place in the refrigerator until nearly set. Whip the egg whites until stiff peaks form, then fold them lightly into the mousse. Transfer into a lightly oiled ring mould and return to the refrigerator to set.

4 To make the chive dressing, simmer the remaining stock, cream and white wine for 10 minutes in a covered saucepan. Add pepper to season. Allow the sauce to cool, then stir in the chives.

5 To serve, turn the ring mould out onto a large plate. Arrange the crayfish tails in the centre and around the mousse. Pour the chive dressing over the mould and top with a teaspoonful of caviar per portion. Make a basket of fresh toast to accompany the mousse. For added luxury, place the crayfish tails around the mould and 250 g (9 oz) caviar in the centre.

Serves 4

SERVE WITH *rosé Champagne, demi-sec Vouvray or Mosel Riesling Kabinett.*

SCALLOPS IN THEIR SHELLS WITH CAVIAR AND ASPARAGUS SAUCE

The combination of scallops, asparagus and caviar works well, so this makes a colourful and attractive dish for a light lunch or starter for a dinner party.

300 g (11 oz) green asparagus, trimmed
30 g (1 oz) butter
8 large scallops
200 ml (7 fl oz) whipping cream
salt and black pepper
4 scallop shells
30–50 g (1–2 oz) Sevruga caviar

1 Preheat the oven to 190°C (375°F/Gas Mark 5). Bring a pan of salted water to the boil. Add the asparagus and cook for 5–7 minutes, until just tender. Drain and cut off the top 5 cm (2 in) of the spears. Set aside for serving. Cut the remaining stems into 2.5 cm (1 in) pieces. If the stems are still hard, boil again for 3–4 minutes. Keep warm.

2 Butter a sheet of tin foil and bake the scallops in the oven for 4 minutes.

3 Put the chopped asparagus stems with the cream into a food processor and blend until it becomes a smooth, creamy consistency. Then take a small saucepan, transfer the asparagus mixture into it and heat gently. Do not allow it to boil. Add salt and pepper to taste.

4 Take four heated plates and place a scallop shell on each one. Then arrange two scallops on each shell. Pour some sauce over each. Place the asparagus tips on top. Then either mix the caviar into the remaining sauce at the last minute or use it to decorate the top.

Serves 4

SERVE WITH NV Champagne, Sancerre/Pouilly-Fumé, white Bordeaux ie Graves or Pessac-Léognan or Riesling Kabinett.

SALMON FILLETS WITH CAVIAR AND SPINACH CREAM SAUCE

If you can obtain sturgeon fillets for this dish, they make a delicious alternative.

30 g (1 oz) butter
550 g (1¼ lb) salmon fillets
salt and black pepper
125 g (4½ oz) Oscietre caviar

Sauce
100 ml (3½ fl oz) dry white wine
2 tbsp dry vermouth (optional)
250 ml (8 fl oz) fish stock
200 ml (7 fl oz) double cream
1 bag (150 g/5 oz) fresh baby spinach
salt and freshly ground black pepper

1 Start to make the sauce by simmering the wine (and vermouth if required) in a saucepan, until it has reduced to 3 tbsp. Add the fish stock and simmer until reduced again to about 6 tbsp.

2 Preheat the grill. Lightly oil a sheet of tin foil. Put a few pieces of butter on the salmon fillets and season with salt and pepper. Place under the grill, cooking them on the second shelf from the top for 3–4 minutes. Turn the fish and grill the other side for 2–3 minutes.

3 Add the cream to the sauce and bring to the boil. Stir in the spinach and seasoning. Divide the sauce between warm plates, placing the salmon on top. Garnish with the caviar.

Serves 4

SERVE WITH *white Bordeaux ie Graves/Pessac-Léognan, white burgundy, Alsace Pinot Blanc.*

LOBSTER SALAD AND CAVIAR

This salad is ideal for the calorie-conscious and those wishing to keep the brain alert.

16 leaves crisp-heart lettuce
16 leaves endive (not the frizzy French lettuce)
3 medium tomatoes
100 g (3½ oz) fine green beans
½ red onion, chopped
balsamic vinegar
1 tbsp virgin olive oil
salt and black pepper
4 cooked lobster tails
100 g (3½ oz) Sevruga caviar

1 Divide and wash the lettuce and endive leaves. Pat dry and put in the refrigerator. Dip the tomatoes in boiling water, then skin them, cut them in half, remove seeds and finely dice.

2 Boil the green beans in salted water for 2–3 minutes. Drain and allow to cool. Chop into 2.5 cm (1 in) lengths into a bowl and add the onion, diced tomato, a few drops of balsamic vinegar, the olive oil, and salt and pepper to taste. Place in the refrigerator for 30 minutes.

3 Split the lobster tails in half lengthways, making sure that the black intestine is removed from the middle of the back. Set aside.

4 Place four lettuce leaves around each plate with the endive leaves on top. Put the split lobster tail flat in the centre. Divide the bean salad between the endive leaves. Put a tsp of caviar in the middle of each lobster tail.

Serves 4

SERVE WITH *Champagne or fine whites from Burgundy or Bordeaux.*

WHOLE SALMON FILLED WITH CAVIAR, IN SPINACH AND PUFF PASTRY

If you can obtain pressed caviar for this dish, it gives a good strong flavour, which enriches the natural taste of the salmon and blends well with the spinach. If not, then Sevruga is fine and will stand up to cooking in the oven without breaking up.

600 g (1 lb 6 oz) fresh spinach
flour, for rolling out the pastry
1 packet (500 g/1¼ lb) frozen puff pastry
100 g (3½ oz) butter, softened
salt and black pepper
1 whole salmon, filleted, boned and without head and tail
125 g (4½ oz) pressed caviar or Sevruga
1 egg

1 Preheat the oven to 250°C (475°F/Gas Mark 9). Wash the spinach and remove any large stalks. In a large saucepan of boiling water, blanch the leaves for 1 minute, then drain and plunge them into cold water. Then drain again and spread them out on kitchen paper to dry.

2 On a floured board, roll out the puff pastry into a square about 8 cm (3 in) longer than the salmon. Cut it into two equal halves and allow to rest for 20 minutes.

3 Take a flat baking dish and line it with buttered tin foil. Put one piece of the pastry onto it. Using the softened butter, generously coat the pastry, then layer it with half of the spinach, leaving at least 3 cm (1¼ in) of the pastry uncovered at the edge. Season well with salt and freshly ground pepper. Next, place one fillet of salmon on top (ie half the fish), with the inside facing upwards. Spread it with the caviar. Place the other fillet on top, with the inside facing downwards, season well and layer with the rest of the spinach and buttered pastry.

4 Using a pastry brush dipped in water, brush around the inside edges of the pastry and then press them together. Trim the pastry neatly around the fish and indent it all round by pressing it down with your fingers. Indent the surface with the tip of a small teaspoon to create the effect of scales and, with a skewer, gently draw in a fish's head and tail, if you like. Beat the egg and brush it over the top of the pastry fish, taking care that the mixture does not run around the base, or the pastry will not rise evenly.

5 Cook in the hot oven for 20 minutes, until the puff pastry is golden brown. Then turn the heat down to 150°C (300°F/Gas Mark 2) and leave for another 15 minutes. Let the pastry settle with the oven door open for a few minutes.

6 This dish can be served hot, or cold as part of a buffet. Using a sharp, serrated knife, cut the salmon into slices, so that all the layers show. This is delicious served with a lemon sauce.

Serves 4

SERVE WITH *top whites from Burgundy or the Rhône.*

HADDOCK SOUFFLE WITH BEURRE BLANC WHITE WINE SAUCE

First, don't be afraid to tackle a soufflé. You can use other fish, such as crab, crayfish or lobster, for this recipe, but be generous with the seasoning or it can be a little bland.

30 g (1 oz) butter
2 tbsp plain flour
500 g (1¼ lb) smoked haddock
(or other fish of your choice)
2 eggs
150 ml (5 fl oz) double cream
beurre blanc white-wine sauce
(see page 142)
50 g (2 oz) caviar of your choice

Stock
1 small onion
1 medium carrot
1 stick of celery
30 g (1 oz) butter
2 tbsp Cognac
4 tbsp dry sherry
300 ml (10 fl oz) dry white wine
juice of 1 lemon
salt and white pepper
bunch of tarragon, chopped

1 Preheat the oven to 200°C (400°F/Gas Mark 6). To make the stock, wash, peel and finely chop the vegetables. Melt the butter in a large saucepan, then lightly fry the vegetables. Heat the Cognac in a ladle, set light to it carefully and pour it immediately over the vegetables. Put out the last flames with the sherry, white wine and lemon juice. Add the salt, pepper and tarragon. Simmer until the stock is reduced by a quarter.

2 To make the soufflé, melt the butter, without discolouring it, in a saucepan. Mix in the flour smoothly with a wooden spoon, over a moderate heat. Gradually work in the stock, stirring continuously until the sauce is smooth and the flour is cooked. Remove from the heat.

3 Dice the raw fish into small pieces. Separate the eggs, lightly beat the yolks, then add them to the sauce with the haddock and cream. In a cold steel/glass bowl, whisk the egg whites until stiff peaks form. Carefully fold the egg whites into the mixture using a plastic spatula, cutting and folding until well mixed.

4 Butter a deep 25 cm (10 in) soufflé dish well, as this will help the soufflé to slide up the sides of the dish and rise well. Pour the mixture into the dish and cook for around 25 minutes, until well risen and brown on top. You can check if it is done by quickly opening the oven and piercing it with a skewer. If the skewer comes out clean, the soufflé should be perfectly cooked.

5 While the soufflé is cooking, make the beurre blanc white-wine sauce (*see* page 142). Just before serving, stir in the caviar. Take the soufflé directly from the oven to the table so that it does not have a chance to collapse. Serve onto heated plates, pouring over the sauce.

Serves 4

SERVE WITH *vintage Champagne, fine, but not overly oaked Chardonnay: Premier or Grand Cru Chablis or top New Zealand Chardonnay.*

TRILOGY OF SMOKED SALMON AND CAVIAR

This dramatic looking dish is a marvellous blend of flavour and texture, lightness and healthy eating, good brain food and not too many calories. This delicious, nutritious dish is ideally made with three types of smoked salmon available at various premier caviar specialist outlets and delicatessen.

Balik Classic
wood-smoked to an old Russian recipe; finely sliced along a whole side, from head to tail

Tsar Nikolaj fillet
the smoked-salmon fillet, cut across into medallions about 1 cm (½ in) thick

Sjomga
very lightly smoked and marinated with dill, then cut into fine slivers

40 g (1½ oz) Tsar Nikolaj smoked-salmon fillet medallions
40 g (1½ oz) Balik Classic (take a long slice and cut it into three)
40 g (1½ oz) Sjomga slivers
50 g (2 oz) mixed salad leaves
15 g (½ oz) Sevruga or Oscietre caviar
15 g (½ oz) salmon or trout eggs
lemon wedges to garnish

Take a large dinner plate. On one side fan out three medallions of smoked-salmon fillet. On the opposite side roll up three sliced portions of Balik smoked salmon into neat rolls, a bit thicker than a cigarette. Slice the dill-flavoured Sjomga crossways into thin slivers and place in a third group on the plate. In the centre of the plate, make a neat mound of mixed salad leaves. Then top the medallions with the caviar and the rolls of salmon with the salmon eggs. Garnish with wedges of lemon.

Serves 1

SERVE WITH *Sancerre/Pouilly-Fumé, white Bordeaux or Riesling Kabinett.*

ROLLED SOLE FILLETS WITH PRAWNS AND TOPPED WITH CAVIAR

This is a way of making a simple ingredient such as sole look more interesting, and is really very easy to prepare. It would also make a good cold dish for a buffet if you multiplied the ingredients.

500 g (1¼ lb) lemon-sole fillets
baby spinach leaves or lettuce
150 ml (5 fl oz) crème fraîche
75 g (3 oz) mayonnaise
1 tsp lemon juice
1–2 tsp Dijon mustard
salt and white pepper
200 g (8 oz) peeled prawns
100 g (3½ oz) caviar

Stock
150 ml (5 fl oz) water
150 ml (5 fl oz) dry white wine
1 bay leaf
1 tbsp parsley, finely chopped
5–6 whole black peppercorns
salt

1 To make the stock, boil the water and white wine, together with the bay leaf, parsley, peppercorns and salt in a saucepan. Cook for 5–8 minutes and allow to cool.

2 Rinse the fish fillets in cold water and dry them. Slice them lengthways.

3 Roll each fillet from tail to head end, then place them side by side in a saucepan big enough to hold them all packed together fairly tightly. Pour the stock over the fish and simmer, covered, for 5–6 minutes. Let the fish cool in the stock.

4 Rinse the spinach or lettuce leaves in cold water, dry them and arrange them on a platter. Take the fish rolls out of the saucepan with a slotted spoon and arrange them in a pyramid on the leaves. Stir the crème fraîche and mayonnaise together with 2–3 tbsp of the stock. Add the lemon juice, mustard, salt and pepper. Pour the sauce over the fish fillets.

5 Scatter the prawns over the fish pyramids, then place a teaspoonful of caviar on the top of each pyramid. Serve the dish with baby new potatoes.

Serves 4

SERVE WITH *vintage Champagne, top white Bordeaux and other fine Sauvignon-Sémillon blends or Mosel Riesling Kabinett.*

MASA'S SCALLOPS WITH CAVIAR

This recipe effectively combines the Japanese culinary practice of using extremely fresh fish with the subtlety of French flavours.

4 Chinese cabbage leaves
12 green asparagus tips
30 g (1 oz) butter
salt and freshly ground black pepper
4 large scallops (without coral)

Beurre blanc white wine sauce
100 g (3½ oz) shallots, finely chopped
300 ml (10 fl oz) white wine
3 tbsp white wine vinegar
3 tbsp double cream
400 g (14 oz) cold butter, diced
3 tbsp chives, finely chopped

8 slices smoked salmon fillet
125 g (4½ oz) Sevruga caviar

1 Preheat the oven to 225°C (425°F/Gas Mark 8). Bring a large saucepan of water to the boil and blanch the cabbage leaves for 1 minute. Drain and plunge them into cold water. Trim the asparagus tips, if necessary, and boil for 3 minutes. Drain, set aside and keep warm.

2 Soften 30 g (1 oz) of butter. Roughly butter the insides of the blanched cabbage leaves. Season the scallops, place them in the centre of the cabbage leaves and wrap them into neat parcels. Brush melted butter over the parcels, then place them in an ovenproof dish. Cook in the oven for approximately 4 minutes.

3 Make the beurre blanc white wine sauce by mixing together the shallots, white wine and vinegar. Simmer until reduced by half and remove from the heat. Stir in the cream and,

whisking vigorously, add the cold butter cubes until the sauce is light and shiny. Season with freshly ground black pepper and mix in the chives. Keep hot in a bowl over a saucepan of hot water (*bain marie*), if necessary, but do not boil again.

4 To serve, place two slices of smoked salmon fillet in the centre of each heated plate. Put three asparagus tips on top, then place the scallop parcel on top of that. Carefully complete the dish by adding 1 tsp of caviar. Pour the sauce around the edge of the dish and serve immediately.

Serves 4

SERVE WITH *Demi-sec Champagne, demi-sec Vouvray, Sauternes/Barsac or Riesling Spätlese.*

LOBSTER COCKTAIL AND CAVIAR

This dish combines lobster, caviar and asparagus in an elegant way.

2 lobsters, cooked (½ per person)
1 Cos lettuce
50 g (2 oz) pasteurized caviar
1 small tin of asparagus, drained
½ orange, with the segments cut in half lengthways and pith and pips removed

Cocktail sauce
4 tbsp light mayonnaise
1 tbsp tomato purée
1 tsp lemon juice
1 tsp Tabasco
1 tbsp Cognac
pinch of paprika
pinch of sugar
salt and black pepper

1 Combine the ingredients for the cocktail sauce and leave in the refrigerator for a few hours to marinate.

2 Take the lobsters from their shells, removing the black intestine down the centre of the backbone and slicing them in half lengthways. Crack the claws and take out the meat.

3 Wash, pat dry on a cloth and trim the lettuce, then fan it around each plate. Spread a pool of cocktail sauce in the middle of the lettuce. Place the lobster tail in the centre, with the claw beside it. Arrange the caviar along the lobster, or in spoonfuls around it. Garnish with the asparagus tips and thin orange segments.

Serves 4

SERVE WITH *fine Chablis or German Riesling.*

MINI CRAB CAKES WITH CAVIAR SAUCE

You can serve these delicious fishcakes either as an appetiser or as a main course with a salad.

250 g (9 oz) crabmeat (tinned crab works well for this dish)
2 shallots, finely chopped
1 tsp lemon rind, grated
1 clove garlic, crushed
2 tsp dill, chopped
salt and freshly ground black pepper
50 g (2 oz) stale breadcrumbs
3 tbsp milk
2 eggs, lightly beaten
light oil for deep-frying (sunflower or soya)

Caviar sauce
1 shallot, finely chopped (or chives, if preferred)
200 ml (7 fl oz) sour cream
2 x 30 g (1 oz) tins Sevruga caviar

1 To make the crab cakes, combine the crab, chopped shallots, lemon rind, garlic, dill, seasoning and breadcrumbs in a bowl. Stir in the milk and beaten eggs. Take 1 tbsp of the mixture, roll it into a ball and flatten it slightly. Do this with the remaining crab mixture, until you have about 12 crab cakes. Heat the oil in a pan and cook the crab cakes until lightly browned. Drain on kitchen paper and keep warm.

2 To make the sauce, mix the shallots (or chives) with the sour cream, then fold in the caviar at the last moment.

Serves 4

SERVE WITH *rosé Champagne, Meursault or Riesling from Alsace or the Mosel.*

STURGEON DISHES

With so many different countries breeding sturgeon we think it is important to give you an idea of how to cook and present this fish. It has a fairly dense, firm flesh, white in colour, whose delicate flavour has been appreciated for centuries. Sturgeon fillets can now be ordered from most fish markets, and small fish are also sold, especially in Italy and France, to the restaurant trade. In addition, sturgeon is sold in tins rather in the style of tuna.

SMOKED STURGEON PATE

As with canned sturgeon, smoked sturgeon should be fairly easy to find.

175 g (6 oz) smoked sturgeon
75 g (3 oz) unsalted butter
4 tsp lemon juice
4 tbsp single cream
pinch of cayenne pepper
pinch of ground nutmeg
1 cucumber, sliced
lemon wedges to garnish

1 Cut up the smoked sturgeon and place in a food processor or blender.

2 In a small saucepan, melt the butter, then add the lemon juice, cream and seasoning. Add this mixture to the blender and process until smooth. Place in a 300 ml (½ pt) bowl and refrigerate. Take out 30 minutes before serving. Garnish with finely sliced cucumber and wedges of lemon or lime. Serve with toast.

Serves 4

SERVE WITH *Alsace Gewurztraminer, demi-sec Vouvray or Riesling Spätlese.*

MARINATED SMOKED STURGEON

A good smoked sturgeon can be delicious, but if not properly smoked it can be rather dry. This recipe ensures that the sturgeon is succulent; it also makes a delicious alternative to smoked salmon or gravadlax.

375 g (13 oz) smoked sturgeon
juice of 1 lemon or lime
150 ml (5 fl oz) virgin olive oil
freshly ground black pepper
chives, finely chopped
dill, finely chopped

1 Spread the smoked sturgeon out on a large dish. Combine the lemon or lime juice with the olive oil and seasoning. Spoon all over the smoked sturgeon, then put into the refrigerator for at least 30 minutes. When you wish to serve it, drain off the excess liquid. Spread the sturgeon slices out on serving plates and sprinkle with chopped chives and dill. Serve with the crusty bread of your choice.

Serves 4

SERVE WITH *Riesling Spätlese, Chablis, Sancerre/Pouilly-Fumé or fino sherry.*

STURGEON STEAKS WITH PASTA
AND CAVIAR SAUCE

No wonder the Romans eulogized about sturgeon! Accompanied by good modern pasta
and a classic sauce, this is a dish fit for a king.

800 g (1¼ lb) sturgeon steaks
(or 750 g/1½ lb if filleted)
150 ml (5 fl oz) fish stock
120 ml (4 fl oz) dry white wine
salt
1 tbsp olive oil
500 g (1¼ lb) fresh pasta, preferably tagliolini or linguini
parsley or dill to garnish

Sauce
450 ml (15 fl oz) double cream
250 g (8 oz) cold unsalted butter, diced
salt and black pepper
juice of ½ lemon
30 g (1 oz) Sevruga caviar

1 Place the sturgeon in a shallow pan.
Add the fish stock with the wine and a pinch
of salt. Bring gently to simmering point, then
remove from the heat, cover and allow to
stand for 5 minutes.

2 Bring a large saucepan of salted water
containing the oil to the boil, so that it is ready
for the pasta.

3 To make the sauce, heat the cream in a
double boiler or saucepan, and bring to the
boil. Remove from the heat and quickly whisk
in the cold cubes of butter, a little at a time,
until the sauce is smooth. Add the seasoning
and lemon juice and keep hot in the double
boiler (or place the saucepan into another
larger pan containing just-simmering water).

4 Cook the pasta following the manufacturer's
instructions, or for about 5 minutes and until
still *al dente*. Drain well and place a mound on
each plate. Fold the caviar into the sauce and
pour over the pasta. Put a sturgeon steak or
fillet on top of each mound and garnish with
parsley or dill sprigs.

Serves 4

*SERVE WITH Alsace Pinot Blanc, top Pinot Bianco
or Pinot Grigio or Premier Cru Chablis.*

MRS BEETON RECIPES

The remaining recipes in this chapter are taken from *Mrs Beeton's Book of Household Management* (first published in 1861, new edition 1888). Mrs Beeton wrote this remarkable book in her early twenties; she died at only twenty-eight years of age, but the book has been updated and is still popular today. It contains over 3,735 recipes and tips on household management. The following excerpts, which describe sturgeon and caviar, are taken directly from the 1888 edition of the book.

"The Sturgeon

This fish commences the sixth of the Linnaean order, and all the species are large, seldom measuring, when full grown, less than three or four feet in length. Its flesh is reckoned extremely delicious, and, in the time of the Emperor Severus, was so highly valued by the ancients, that it was brought to the table by servants crowned with coronets, and preceded by a band of music. It is an inhabitant of the Baltic, the Mediterranean, the Caspian and the Black Sea, and of the Danube, the Volga, the Don, and other large rivers. It is abundant in the rivers of North America, and is occasionally taken in the Thames, as well as in the Eske and the Eden. It is one of those fishes considered as royal property. It is from its roe that caviare is prepared. Its flesh is delicate, firm and white, but is rare in the London market."

"The Sterlet is a smaller species of sturgeon, found in the Caspian Sea and some Russian rivers. It also is greatly prized on account of the delicacy of its flesh."

"Estimate of the Sturgeon by the Ancients

By the ancients, the flesh of this fish was compared to the ambrosia of the immortals. The poet Martial passes a high eulogium upon it, and assigns it a place on the luxurious tables of the Palatine Mount. If we may credit a modern traveller in China, the people of that country generally entirely abstain from it, and the sovereign of the Celestial Empire confines it to his own kitchen, or dispenses it to only a few of his greatest favourites."

BAKED STURGEON (ESTURGEON ROTI AU VIN BLANC)

1 small sturgeon
salt and pepper to taste
1 small bunch of herbs
the juice of ½ lemon
¼ lb butter
1 pint of white wine

Cleanse the fish thoroughly, skin it, and split it along the belly without separating it; have ready a large baking-dish, in which to lay the fish, sprinkle over the seasoning and herbs very finely minced, and moisten it with the lemon-juice and wine. Place the butter in small pieces over the whole of the fish, put it in the oven, and baste frequently; brown it nicely, and serve with its own gravy.

Time. – Nearly 1 hour. Average Cost. 6d to 1s. per lb.

Seasonable from April to September.

ROAST STURGEON (ESTURGEON ROTI)

Veal stuffing
buttered paper
the tail-end of a sturgeon

Cleanse the fish, bone and skin it; make a nice veal stuffing (see Forcemeat, right), and fill with it the part where the bones came from; roll it in buttered paper, bind it up firmly with tape, like a fillet of veal, and roast in a Dutch oven before a clear fire. Serve with good brown gravy (see page 149), or plain melted butter.

Time. – About 1 hour. Average Cost, 6d. to 1s. per lb.

Seasonable from April to September.

Note. – Sturgeon may be plain-boiled, and served with Dutch Sauce (see below). The fish is very firm, and requires long boiling.

DUTCH SAUCE (SAUCE HOLLANDAISE)

½ teaspoonful of flour
2 oz of butter
2 tablespoonfuls of vinegar
2 tablespoonfuls of water
the yolks of 2 eggs
the juice of ½ lemon
salt to taste

Put all the ingredients, except the lemon juice, into a stewpan; set it over the fire, and keep continually stirring. When it is sufficiently thick, take it off, as it should not boil. If, however, it happens to curdle, strain the sauce through a tammy, add the lemon juice, and serve. Tarragon vinegar may be used instead of plain, and, by many, is considered far preferable.

Average Cost, 6d.

BROWN GRAVY
(JUS DE VIANDE)

2 oz butter

2 large onions

2 lbs of shin of beef

2 small slices of lean bacon (if at hand)

salt and whole pepper to taste

3 cloves

2 quarts of water

For thickening

2 oz butter

3 oz flour

Put the butter into a stewpan; set this on the fire, throw in the onions cut in rings, and fry them a light brown; then add the beef and bacon, which should be cut into small pieces; season, and pour in a teacupful of water, stirring the contents. Now fill up with water in the above proportion; let it boil up, then draw it to the side of the fire to simmer very gently for three or four hours; strain, and when cold take off all the fat. In thickening this gravy, melt 1½ oz of butter in a stewpan, add 2 oz of flour, and stir till of a light-brown colour; add it to the strained gravy, and boil it up quickly. This gravy may be made to look nice with a little drop of Sutton's Browning.

FORCEMEAT
(FARCE DE VEAU)

1 lb of veal

1 lb of fat bacon

salt, cayenne pepper

and pounded mace to taste

a very little nutmeg, the same of chopped lemon-peel

½ a teaspoonful of chopped parsley

½ a teaspoonful of minced savoury herbs

1 or 2 eggs

Chop the veal and bacon together, and put them in a mortar with the other ingredients mentioned above. Pound well, and bind with one or two eggs which have been previously beaten and strained. Work the whole well together, and the forcemeat will be ready for use. If it is not to be eaten immediately, omit the herbs and parsley, as these would prevent it from keeping. Mushrooms or truffles may be added.

FOOD, SEX AND BEAUTY

Caviar is light, full of vitamins and protein, low in calories and almost a complete food in itself. It is perfect if you are feeling under the weather or are convalescing. The following chart offers a nutritional breakdown and calorie count per kg of caviar:

	CAVIAR	PRESSED CAVIAR	STURGEON
Protein	26–30.4	36.2	17.8
Fats	15.7–16.3	20.0	9.5
Minerals/salts	1.2–4.4	1.8–7.1	1.0
Water	52.7–53.3	31.4–36.7	71.7
Calories	2,700	3,200	1,610

Russia has known of the health benefits of caviar for centuries; even today it is used to prevent rickets in children and is given to patients after surgery. In the past, the oils were extracted from the eggs and drunk, just as Western Europeans would drink cod-liver oil, for the vitamins. Some Russian men still drink the oils to line their stomach before a drinking binge as caviar contains acetylcholine, which is linked to increased tolerance to alcohol. The last Tsar of Russia was so convinced of the health benefits of caviar that he made his children eat a spoonful every day. The ingrates did not like it much, so their chef combined it with mashed banana and served it on French bread.

One London pharmacist used to inject oil from caviar into capsules to take as a vitamin supplement. A spoonful of caviar is certainly more delicious than a vitamin pill and probably just as beneficial.

RIPE FOR SEDUCTION

Because of its rarity, expense (and, in the past, the difficulty of transporting and therefore getting hold of it) and its delicious flavour, caviar has always played an important role in the art of seduction – whether it be to impress lovers, politicians or power-brokers.

Many myths have been spun around this exotic delicacy through the ages. Ancient Russian, Indian and Persian poems all refer to the aphrodisiac powers of this unique egg, which was used for its "exciting virtues" and the passions it can arouse. It is said that consuming good caviar is like making love: the first time is a little strange, but after several times you can't get enough! And it is the perfect food for lovers – light to eat, full of good health – and eating caviar is a sensuous adventure in itself.

It may seem a little bizarre but the spinal marrow, or *vesiga*, in the backbone of the sturgeon is also considered an aphrodisiac. In China it is pulverized and given to a bride, because it is thought to bring good fortune and fertility. The *vesiga* is also dried and plaited, and used in special soups.

KEEP YOUNG AND BEAUTIFUL

The beauty benefits of caviar and its oil are well reported, so it is no surprise that several cosmetic companies use it as an ingredient in their face and body product ranges. In 1964 the cosmetic company Ingrid Millet of France began to formalize the benefits of caviar, basing its research on the similarity in composition between a sturgeon egg and the human skin cell. It produces a full range of beauty products using caviar oils. The company makes strong claims for the anti-ageing properties of caviar extracts. Ingrid Millet uses the best-quality caviar and is just as concerned as sturgeon producers and caviar retailers about the future of the sturgeon. The Swiss cosmetics company La Prairie is also famous for its caviar-based products.

Caviar has also been used for face packs, made into face and body creams, hair tonics and even a cuticle cream. Parts of the male sturgeon have been put to good use – in Russia even the testes were made into a balm for healing burns.

THE LANGUAGE
OF CAVIAR

Almas *Golden caviar*

Either the eggs of the albino sturgeon or those of an Oscietre sturgeon of at least 60 years of age. The flavours respectively are light and delicate or creamy and subtle. See also page 46.

Beluga *Huso huso*

These large sturgeon are now extremely rare. Beluga eggs are the largest and are light grey to nearly black with a fine skin that melts in the mouth. The flavour is delicately fishy. See also page 48.

Kaluga *Huso dauricus*

One of the largest sturgeon species comes from the Amur and Liman Rivers in China. Commonly known as Kaluga, it resembles the Beluga and matures at around eighteen to twenty years of age. An average fish weighs around 80 kg (176 lb) and is about 2.3 m (7½ ft) in length. The eggs from the Kaluga may be acceptable if they are fresh, but owing partly to the fishing methods used – whereby fish are kept in boats for several days before reaching the fishing stations – they are often not processed to a consistent quality, can be very salty and do not keep well. The eggs are similar in size to those of a young Oscietre and are processed with up to 6 per cent salt.

Malossol

Malossol means "lightly salted" in Russian, although today the term has come to mean any high-quality caviar. Traditionally only eggs that are in prime condition are prepared and labelled in this way. It takes great expertise to judge at what stage a sturgeon's eggs are absolutely right for this process, which should not contain more than 2.8–3 per cent salt. In the US and Iran pure salt is used, but in Russia and some eastern countries a small amount of legally permitted borax is added, which many experts believe helps to preserve the caviar and enhances its natural flavour by sweetening it slightly.

Oscietre *Acipenser gueldenstaedti*

These sturgeon produce the widest range of eggs. The eggs fade from dark golden to a pale amber as the fishes age and tend to have a subtle "walnuts and cream" flavour. See also page 52.

Pasteurized caviar

The Americans were pasteurizing caviar at the end of the 1800s, and Russia went into pasteurizing caviar seriously around the time of the First World War. Because of disruptions to sturgeon fishing, particularly due to cold weather and lack of refrigeration, they used their existing stocks of caviar rather than lose their established markets. They poured the eggs into huge 500 litre (110 gallon) barrels, covered the tops and left them in a very hot room to cook.

Today's methods are more effective. Caviar is put into 30 g (1 oz), 60 g (2 oz) or 110 g (4 oz) glass jars, sealed, then placed in water baths at a constant temperature of about 60°C (140°F).

The length of pasteurization depends on the size of the jar; small jars are left for about thirty minutes; larger ones for about forty-five. Methods are also being developed to pasteurize caviar in ovens, as this reduces the risk of water rusting the metal lids or getting into the caviar. The jars are normally labelled in the traditional colours: Sevruga with a red label, Oscietre with a yellow label and Beluga with a blue one. If pasteurization is correctly carried out there should be no discernible change in the eggs' flavour, although they can become firmer.

Pasteurized caviar will keep unrefrigerated for up to one year but, once opened, needs to be consumed within a few days.

Pressed caviar

This has a very salty, fishy taste. In the past pressing was the first known method of preserving sturgeon roe, so references to caviar consumed before the twentieth century generally refer to pressed caviar, except where it was locally supplied as a fresh product. Nowadays it is normally made from Sevruga or Oscietre that has been damaged in processing, or from a mixture of eggs that have been left over from several different batches. Immature or overripe eggs are also used for this purpose. It takes 6 kg (13 lb) to make 1 kg (2¼ lb) of pressed caviar.

The roe is washed, sieved and put into vats with pure salt. Hot water is then added, to ensure that the salt reaches all parts of the egg mass, and the mixture is left for a couple of hours. Then it is pressed in a screw- or lever-press until most of the oils have been extracted. The roe then forms a dense mass which can be sliced or spread. This makes it highly suitable for certain recipes and it can withstand a certain amount of cooking. It

also freezes quite well. Before refrigeration, pressed caviar was very expensive, because it could be preserved for a long period. Today it should cost around the same as Sevruga, or slightly less.

The Russian term for pressed caviar is *payusnaya ikra* – the name deriving from the Russian word pay, which means to divide and share according to an agreement. When fishermen had caught sturgeon, they processed, pressed and divided the eggs between them, according to the ranking of those in the boat. The most popular pressed caviar was reputed to come from Saljany in Azerbaijan. This was pressed into 480 kg (1,060 lb) barrels, then sealed with paraffin wax to keep out the air. It was then sold in 15 kg (33 lb), 20 kg (44 lb) or 25 kg (55 lb) wooden casks, some of which were highly decorated and carved and have now become collectors' items. When a customer wished to buy caviar, the cask was opened, the caviar removed according to the weight required, and the lid replaced. In the past caviar importers were obliged to take a certain quantity when ordering caviar, but today – because of its rarity and value – this is no longer the case.

Pressed caviar is difficult to find outside Russia, but many connoisseurs claim that it is their favourite form of caviar, as it has such a dense, strong flavour. It is definitely an acquired taste.

Schipp *Acipenser nudiventris*

Schipp is the result of cross-breeding a Sevruga with a Sterlet. It is sometimes sold commercially, but is usually packaged as either Sevruga or Oscietre, depending on the egg size, although its eggs are often less firm than those of its parent fish.

Sevruga *Acipenser stellatus*

These are the smallest sturgeon whose grey-black eggs are fine grained. They taste distinctively salty. Sevruga is the least expensive, yet highly prized for the unique flavour. See also page 50.

Sterlet *Acipenser ruthenus*

The Sterlet is similar to, but smaller than, the average Sevruga and has been known to reach 1.25 m (4 ft) and weigh 16 kg (35 lb), although normally it does not grow to more than 1 m (3¼ ft) and weighs 6–6.5 kg (13–14 lb).

In the past Sterlet, which is mainly a river sturgeon, accounted for over 50 per cent of the catch in the mouth of the Volga River. Fifty years ago 700 tonnes were caught in an average year. Now they are very rare. The Sterlet is still found in the Danube and is increasing there, mainly due to improved pollution controls. The largest remaining population is in Yugoslavia, followed by Bulgaria, Romania, Czechoslovakia and Hungary. Although it is no longer caught in commercial quantities, Sterlet is a very important fish as far as propagation is concerned, breeding and cross-breeding successfully in warm water with other species of sturgeon, which makes it vital for the future of the species.

The Sterlet is often mentioned historically, having been popular at all kinds of feasts and banquets, especially as caviar soup.

OTHER STURGEON SPECIES

There are estimated to be at least thirty species of sturgeon still in existence, but this is not easy to establish, because some species have cross-bred; others have changed their habitat; others have evolved and now remain in the river systems and never return to the sea, or vice-versa.

Sturgeon farming is expanding in many countries, including Russia, Germany, Hungary, France, Italy, Spain, Portugal, Israel, Romania, Iran, the US, Chile, Argentina, Uruguay and China. Two of the principal types of sturgeon being farmed are described below. You may also come across the Atlantic sturgeon (*Acipenser oxyrhynchus*), which is found in the Mediterranean and the Black Sea, off the Atlantic coast of North America, and in Icelandic, Russian and British waters.

Italian sturgeon *Acipenser naccarii*

Italy has its own native species of sturgeon, which is still occasionally found in the Adriatic Sea. Up until fairly recently it was prevalent in the Po and other northern Italian rivers, but, unfortunately, only a few sturgeon are found there now. A great deal of sturgeon farming is taking place in Italy around Venice and in Lombardy, where they are cross-breeding with the Siberian sturgeon.

Siberian sturgeon *Acipenser baeri*

This is the most important fish for breeding and aquaculture and is being widely used in northern Europe, Hungary, France and Spain for propagation of the species with the native sturgeon, which remains in these areas. France is allowed to breed only from this fish, as it is the closest to their indigenous sturgeon. Germany and Hungary are more flexible and, as they have a greater variety of native species, their farmers may propagate from a selection of sturgeon.

OTHER FISH EGGS

As we have seen, the best caviar comes from sturgeon living in the Caspian Sea, which has the most highly valued flavour deriving from its habitat, climate and traditional fishing methods. There are many other parts of the world producing caviar (such as southwest France where *caviare d'Acquitaine* or "French sturgeon roe" is produced), but they never consistently equal the quality and taste of Caspian caviar.

By law, in most countries fish eggs should only be labelled as "caviar" if they come from sturgeon caught in the Caspian Sea or the Baltic States. Other fish eggs should have the name of the fish prior to the word "caviar" – for example, "lumpfish caviar" or "salmon caviar".

Most fish and shellfish eggs can be processed and consumed, so we have given below a brief description of some of the main fish eggs found commercially. Among those that we have not described are herring, flying fish, pike, carp, pollack, flounder, mackerel and other white fish eggs. Some crab eggs are also edible.

Cod's roe

This is popular either as freshly smoked roe served on its own with toast or more commonly as the main ingredient of *taramasalata* or *tarama* – a Greek pâté, made from cod's roe, bread, oil, garlic and seasoning. Cod's roe comes in a reddish, orange mass of dense, tiny eggs, in a flattish oval shape. Most fishmongers stock smoked cod's roe.

As with most fish eggs, the soft roe is highly nutritious and easy to digest; it is often fried or poached on toast. The traditional English nanny often gave this to children as it was "very good for them". It is normally purchased in tins.

Fake fish eggs

Many countries produce fake eggs, made out of fish products combined with oils, gelatine and flavourings, which when processed resemble fish eggs. Even Russia makes an artificial protein caviar out of non-fish ingredients, which include casein, modified proteins, hens' egg yolks, gelatine, flavourings and dyes. The size and colour of "egg" can be made to resemble almost any fish egg from salmon to sturgeon.

Japan claims to make an artificial fish egg resembling caviar that will sustain cooking. There is even a low-calorie kosher variety produced in Israel made out of fish, vegetable oils and other natural ingredients (artificial colourings are apparently not used).

Lobster eggs

The coral of the lobster (which is its roe) is useful for flavour and colour when it is pounded or finely chopped into sauces.

Lobster eggs can be taken from the lobster, spread out on a baking sheet and dried at a moderate heat in a fan-oven. They can then be used to enhance the flavour and colour of stocks and fish sauces or sprinkled over fish dishes, rather like poppy seed.

Løgrum

This is a flat fish caught mainly in Scandinavian waters. The eggs are normally a very pale creamy colour, and slightly smaller than those of lumpfish. Løgrum has a delicate flavour, which makes it a popular egg in Scandinavia; it also has a substantial market in Canada. It is even produced in a tube as pâté for children.

Lumpfish eggs

As its name suggests, this is an ugly, lumpy fish, found mainly in Scandinavian waters. It grows up to 35–60 cm (14–24 in) in length and weighs 2–7 kg (4–15½ lb); 15–30 per cent of its body weight consists of eggs. The eggs are a small-grain roe, which come in a whole rainbow of different colours, which are normally dyed dark grey/black or red to resemble Sevruga or salmon roe.

Lumpfish is widely used as a garnish for soups and canapés, instead of authentic caviar. The eggs have a mildly fishy, salty taste and are slightly crunchy. They can also be processed with different flavours. Similar "kaviar" eggs are processed from the sea hare, sea owl and other species.

Mujjol shikran *Eurocaviar*

Invented and produced in Spain, this is a mixture of 40 per cent grey mullet eggs, mixed with herring and cod's roe, then processed to resemble caviar, although the colour is blackish-brown. Due to its method of manufacture it can withstand temperatures of up to 100°C (212°F), so it can be a useful addition to recipes that require cooking. It has both a market and a distinctive flavour all its own, and is currently produced in quantities upwards of 100 tonnes per annum. It is packaged in glass jars, freezes well and is a fraction of the price of real caviar.

Mullet eggs

These are the oldest recorded dried and processed eggs, predating sturgeon. Today they are still widely sold as "botarga" (*botargue* or *potargue* in France, the spelling depending on the country concerned). The eggs are salted, pressed and dried, then normally preserved in a translucent wax casing. The best-quality eggs are a golden-orange colour, with no flaws or discolouration when held up to the light.

Mullet eggs come in a dense, pressed mass and are eaten, finely sliced as an appetizer or soaked in olive oil on bread. They have an intensely fishy flavour, which is considered a great delicacy in many countries.

Salmon eggs

These are large, naturally orange/red eggs about the size of a small pea. They have a strong salmon, "yolky" flavour and should pop in the mouth. The eggs should be a good round shape and should not break when squeezed. The roe is often pasteurized and, if correctly processed, this should not affect its flavour. In fact, it is often difficult to tell whether or not it has been pasteurized, because of the consistency of the eggs. Salmon eggs freeze well, although we recommend that they are defrosted in the refrigerator to prevent them from rupturing.

Salmon roe is usually sold in glass jars of 50 g (2 oz), 100 g (3½ oz) or 150 g (5 oz), or in plastic catering buckets of 1.5–5 kg (3¼–11 lb) in size. Its normal salt content is 3–4.5 per cent, and its shelf life is generally three to four months, although pasteurized eggs will keep for longer.

Most salmon are caught in Alaskan, Canadian and Russian waters. Japan and Russia are by far the largest producers and consumers of salmon eggs (several thousand tonnes). Various species of salmon are used for their eggs, but in Europe the most common type is Keta (*Oncorhynchus keta*) and in the US, chum, pink or sockeye.

In Europe salmon eggs are often used as a garnish, for canapés or eaten with pancakes and sour cream as an alternative to caviar. They form a popular sushi and sashimi ingredient.

Sea-urchin eggs

One of the most expensive seafood eggs weight for weight comes from oursin, which is a type of black, spiny sea urchin considered a delicacy among connoisseurs. These sea urchins are now a protected species in some Mediterranean waters. They are seasonally eaten in the winter months, having been collected from deep rocky waters. When cut open, they reveal a bright orange mass of very small eggs along the inside edges of the shell, rather like five long tongues.

Sea-urchin eggs have a strong taste of iodine and a soft, slightly grainy texture. Apart from being consumed raw, they blend well with scrambled eggs, omelettes or even made into soufflés in their own shells.

Trout eggs

The trout egg is a smaller-grained orange egg, about half the size of a salmon egg, and is usually processed from the salmon trout. Although the eggs of other trout are edible, they may not have the same depth of colour.

One fishing friend of ours takes the eggs from the trout she catches, soaks them in milk for an hour, then rinses them in water several times, removing all the membranous bits. She then adds salt and a little sugar, and drains off as much liquid as possible, first through a sieve and then on kitchen paper. Next she places the eggs in a glass bowl and presses them down with a weight for twenty-four hours in the refrigerator. They are then served, spread on crisp buttered toast.

Tuna eggs

There are many species of tuna all over the world. In Europe tuna is caught off the west coasts of Sardinia and Sicily and in central Mediterranean waters. In the 1930s it was fashionable to fish for "tunny fish" in Scarborough, the well-known seaside resort on the northeast coast of England. Spawning occurs from April until June, when water temperatures become warmer. Tuna always use the same route to their spawning grounds, so the fishermen know where to place their nets to catch the fish. When the tuna are landed they are immediately cut up and processed, either for canning or for fresh meat. Traditionally the eggs were divided among the fishermen, taken home and salted, pressed for several days and then left to hang in a dry, well-ventilated place for two or three months.

Today tuna eggs are vacuum-packed, which helps to retain their taste and fragrance. They should be taken out of their container a couple of hours before serving. Like most other fish eggs, they are very rich in mineral salts and proteins and are a rare, much-prized delicacy, sought-after by gourmets throughout the world. The Italians grate tuna eggs over pasta dishes.

INDEX